GOOD NEWS STUDIES

Consulting Editor: Robert J. Karris, O.F.M.

1. Call to Discipleship: A Literary Study of Mark's Gospel
   by Augustine Stock, O.S.B.
2. Becoming Human Together
   The Pastoral Anthropology of St. Paul
   by Jerome Murphy-O'Connor, O.P.
3. Light of All Nations
   Studies on the Church in New Testament Research
   by Daniel Harrington, S.J.
4. Palestinian Judaism and the New Testament
   by Martin McNamara, M.S.C.
5. The Apocalypse: The Perennial Revelation of Jesus Christ
   by Eugenio Corsini
   Translated and Edited by Francis Moloney, S.D.B.
6. St. Paul's Corinth: Texts & Archaeology
   by Jerome Murphy-O'Connor, O.P.
7. A New Look at Preaching
   Walter J. Burghardt/Raymond E. Brown, et. al.
8. A Galilean Rabbi and His Bible
   Jesus' Use of the Interpreted Scripture of His Time
   by Bruce D. Chilton
9. The Unity of Luke's Theology: An Analysis of Luke-Acts
   by Robert F. O'Toole, S.J.
10. Experiencing the Good News: New Testament as Communication
    by James M. Reese, O.S.F.S.
11. Leadership in Paul
    by Helen Doohan
12. Gospel Love: A Narrative Theology
    by John Navone, S.J.
13. Christ is Community: The Christologies of the New Testament
    by Jerome H. Neyrey, S.J.
14. The Sermon on the Mount: Proclamation and Exhortation
    by Jan Lambrecht, S.J.
15. People of the Resurrection
    by Lionel Swain
16. The Early Christians: Their World Mission & Self-Discovery
    by Ben Meyer
17. God Makes Me Laugh: A New Approach to Luke
    by Joseph A. Grassi
18. Reckoning With Romans: A Contemporary Reading of Paul's Gospel
    by Brendan Byrne, SJ

Other Titles in Preparation

Q

The Sayings of Jesus

by Ivan Havener, O.S.B.

With a Reconstruction of Q
by Athanasius Polag

A Michael Glazier Book
THE LITURGICAL PRESS
Collegeville, Minnesota

About the Author

Ivan Havener, O.S.B., earned his doctoral degree at the University of Munich where he concentrated on New Testament studies. Among his publications is a commentary on the minor letters of Paul for the new Collegeville Bible Commentary series.

A Michael Glazier Book
published by
THE LITURGICAL PRESS

Where indicated, the Bible text in this publication is from, or derived from, the Revised Standard Version of the Bible, copyrighted 1946, 1952, © 1971, 1973 by the Division of Christian Education of the National Council of the Churches of Christ in the U.S.A., and used by permission.

Typography by Connie Runkel. Text designed by Michael Truax.

2	3	4	5	6	7	8	9

Library of Congress Cataloging-in-Publication Data

Havener, Ivan, 1943–
    Q : the sayings of Jesus / by Ivan Havener. With A reconstruction of Q / by Athanasius Polag.
       p. cm. — (Good news studies ; v. 19)
    "A Michael Glazier book."
    "A reconstruction of Q" translated into English from: Fragmenta Q.
    Reprint. Originally published: Wilmington, Del. : M. Glazier,
1987.
    Includes bibliographical references and indexes.
    ISBN 0-8146-5441-X
    1. Bible. N.T. Gospels—Criticism, interpretation, etc. 2. Q
hypothesis (Synoptics criticism) I. Fragmenta Q. English. 1990.
II. Title. III. Series.
BS2555.2.H26   1990
226'.06—dc20   90-42837
                                   CIP

MEINEM HOCHVEREHRTEN
LEHRER
HERRN PROF. DR.
OTTO KUSS
IN DANKBARKEIT

Table of Contents

Foreword 11

Part One: An Introduction to Q 17
   The Q Hypothesis 19
   The Letter Designation "Q" 28
   The Genre and Oral Nature of Q 29
   Date and Place of Composition of Q 42
   God in Q 45
   The Kingdom of God 50
      Presence of the Kingdom 50
      Future Manifestation of the Kingdom 53
      Imminent Judgment and Its Delay 57
   John the Baptist's Relation to Jesus in Q 62
   The Person and Role of Jesus in Q 67
      Jesus as the Prophetic Son of God 68
      Jesus as the Son of Man 72
      Jesus as the Agent of Wisdom 78
      Jesus as Lord 83
   Spirit in Q 86

The Q Community and Its Mission 91

Epilogue 104

Part Two: The Text of Q

Preface 111

Translator's Note 115

Table of Q Contents 117

TEXT OF Q: SAYINGS OF THE LORD JESUS

A. Introduction 123

B. Sermon on the Mount 125

C. John the Baptist 128

D. Mission of the Disciples 129

E. On Prayer 132

F. Controversies 132

G. On Acknowledgement 136

H. On Proper Concerns 137

I. Parables 140

J. On the Responsibility of Disciples 144

K. On Judgment 144

Appendices

Appendix I.

Texts Possibly Pertaining to Q 147

Appendix II.

Introductory Phrases Possibly Pertaining to Q .. 149

Appendix III.

Marcan Passages Parallel to Q 153

Synopsis of Mark and Q Traditions 160

Appendix IV.
Septuagint Passages Related to Q 163

Select Bibliography

A. Non-Technical Works on Q
   in English (Annotated) 167
B. Technical Works on Q in English
   (or English Translation) 169
C. Major Foreign Language Works on Q 170

Indices

Index of Ancient Writings 172
Index of Selected Topics, Persons and Places 174
Index of Modern Authors 176

Foreword

This introduction to the text and theology of Q has grown out of a practical concern to provide undergraduate college students and graduate students without a knowledge of Greek with a responsible reconstruction in English translation of the text of Q, as it was used by Matthew and Luke in the composition of their Gospels. Up to now there have been introductions to the content of Q but not printed together with a reconstruction of the text. Students have generally been required to look up several parallel passages in Matthew and Luke in order to get some idea of what Q was like. Needless to say, that is an inconvenient way to approach Q, even with use of a book of gospel parallels. This work seeks to remedy that situation.

Because Q's theology and its written expression is either contemporary with the Apostle Paul's writings or possibly even antedates Paul's, we have in Q one of the earliest writings, if not the earliest writing in Christianity. Its content is almost entirely different from what we find in Paul, and its view of Christianity challenges us to rethink the very beginnings of Christianity itself. This is justification enough for us to become familiar with Q.

Even though all that we have of Q is found in the Gospels of Matthew and Luke, Q is not a biblical document per se. Its parts were used anew in different contexts by Matthew and Luke, thus destroying the fiber of Q's own theological point of view. A careful reading of the text of Q will disclose numerous ideas that break or clash with our contemporary understanding of Christian orthodoxy. No attempt is made here to defend such ideas, merely to set them forth as they seem to have existed in Q thought.

This book is divided into two parts. The first part presents an introduction to Q and its main theological points, as well as a look at the community that produced the Q document. No effort is made here to argue all points of view that have been raised concerning almost all areas of Q theology and concerning the question of the very existence of Q itself. Such a task would be enormous and result in the kind of book that would not best serve the audience this is intended to serve. Footnotes have purposely been used sparingly and the bibliography is geared to English works, but since so many important scholarly works on Q have appeared in German, some of the more important of these have been included as well.

The second part of this book is a translation of Athanasius Polag's reconstruction of the Q text as it was used by Matthew and Luke. The rationale for that text is explained by Polag himself in his introduction which is provided by us in the pages preceding the text of Q in Part Two of this work.

The choice of Polag's reconstruction is easy to explain in that it is the only recent attempt to reproduce Q's text in its original Greek that has been published. Not all of Polag's exegetical decisions have been greeted with enthusiasm by other scholars of Q, especially his decision to include some passages that are found only in Matthew or only in Luke, but it still remains one of the best scholarly attempts to reconstruct Q to date and provides students, in any case, with a good idea of what Q was like as a document.

Scholarly research on both the text of Q and its interpretation continues. There is currently, for instance, a Society of Biblical Literature seminar on Q that under the chairmanship of James M. Robinson is painstakingly reconstructing the Greek text of Q anew, and Robinson himself is preparing a technical commentary on Q for the prestigious *Hermeneia* commentary series.

This book, however, attempts to bring some of the treasures of Q research to a broader audience and even, perhaps, to spark some interest in the history of early Christianity and of the New Testament as well.

A special word of thanks is in order to Michael Glazier whose enthusiasm and patience have encouraged me to undertake and complete this project. I am also grateful to Athanasius Polag, O.S.B., and Neukirchener Verlag for permission to translate into English the Greek text of Q prepared by Father Polag. Gratitude is also due to Mrs. Brenda Levinski, Secretary-Receptionist of the Saint John's University Department of Theology for her gracious, efficient assistance in typing and preparing the manuscript and to Mr. Jeffrey Hutson, for proofreading the text. Finally I wish to thank my own students of a seminar on Q held the spring term of 1980 in the Saint John's School of Theology. They provided me with the inspiration for this work.

Transitus of our	*Ivan Havener, O.S.B.*
Holy Father Benedict	Saint John's University
March 21, 1986	Collegeville, Minnesota

PART ONE
An Introduction to Q
by
Ivan Havener

An Introduction to Q

In the preface to his Gospel, Luke the Evangelist indicates that he has used various sources in the composition of his work:

> Inasmuch as many have undertaken to compile a narrative of the things which have been accomplished among us, just as they were delivered to us by those who from the beginning were eyewitnesses and ministers of the word, it seemed good to me also, having followed all things closely for some time past, to write an orderly account for you, most excellent Theophilus, that you may know the truth concerning the things of which you have been informed. Luke 1:1-4 (RSV)

Since only four biblical Gospels have come down to us, the phrase, "many have undertaken to compile a narrative," raises the question of who these "many" were. Was Luke exaggerating or did he know of several other Gospels or was he referring to smaller collections of gospel stories or sayings of Jesus?

We cannot answer this question with certainty, but the possibility that other "Gospels" may have existed has given rise to some imaginative fiction in our own times, such as

Irving Wallace's best selling *The Word*[1] and the less well known work by Robert L. Duncan (= James Hall Roberts), entitled *The "Q" Document.*[2] Both of these works appeal to the present day desire to learn more about Jesus, to get a clearer picture and understanding of the historical person.

This desire has, no doubt, been influenced, at least in part, by the discovery of post-biblical gospel writings, like the fragment of the Gospel of Peter and the sayings collection now known as the Gospel of Thomas and remnants from other documents.[3] While these discoveries may contain some traditions that are as ancient as those in the biblical Gospels and some sayings that may even go back to Jesus himself, the present form of these writings is not as old as the biblical Gospels themselves.

There is, however, the possibility that behind our present Gospels lies a substantial document that tells of the preaching and teaching of Jesus and that interprets the meaning of his person in a way that is significantly different from the portrayals of Jesus in the biblical Gospels. This "document" no longer exists in an independent form but has been utilized by the Evangelists Matthew and Luke in the composition of their Gospels. With painstaking care this document can be reconstructed from these two Gospels, even though the precise length and wording of this document in the form received by Matthew and Luke is not known.[4] The material that belongs to it has undoubtedly gone through various stages of development. Its beginnings are to be located in the ministry of Jesus but the form of the document that lay before Matthew and Luke clearly reflects also the later

[1](New York: Simon and Schuster, 1972).

[2](New York: Ballantine Books, 1964).

[3]These documents are conveniently collected and given excellent brief introductions by Ron Cameron, ed., *The Other Gospels. Non-Canonical Gospel Texts* (Philadelphia: The Westminster Press, 1982).

[4]Since Matthew used nearly all of the Gospel of Mark in the writing of his own Gospel, it seems likely that he probably incorporated all or most of Q as it was known to him. If this was, in fact, the case, we know that Q must not have been much lengthier than what is presented in Part Two of this work, where Q is reconstructed in the form it was used by Matthew and Luke.

theological perspectives of the community of Christians that produced it over a period of thirty to forty years.

This document that now lies hidden behind Matthew and Luke is commonly known as the "Q document," the "Q source" or simply as "Q." The nature of this document and what it says theologically is the purpose of this introductory essay. This introduction is followed, in turn, by a reconstruction of the fragments of the final redaction of Q, as proposed by Athanasius Polag. [5] References to Q within the introductory essay follow Polag's numbering of the sayings, so that Q passages can quickly be located and identified for further examination.

The Q Hypothesis

In order to understand what the Q hypothesis is and where it comes from, we need to take a look at the relationship of the first three Gospels (Matthew, Mark and Luke) to one another. These three Gospels tell the story of Jesus in a similar way in contrast to the Gospel of John which has a very different story line. This similarity of the first three Gospels is so strong that often the very same words, even the same word order, are used. As a result, we call these Gospels of Matthew, Mark and Luke "Synoptic Gospels" because they bear the same basic perspective.

When we look more closely at the relationship of these Synoptic Gospels to one another, we find that there is a definite literary connection among them. This can best be seen by taking a unit of material or a "pericope" and comparing the three texts with one another. For the most precise comparison, of course, this must make use of the texts in their original Greek wording, but even in the English translation (especially in the Revised Standard Version) enough of this similarity comes through to make our point; for

---

[5] *Fragmenta Q. Textheft zur Logienquelle* (Neukirchen-Vluyn: Neukirchener Verlag, 1979; 2nd ed. with corrections, 1982).

example, let us look at the beginning words of the passion narrative that introduce the final suffering of Jesus:

THE CONSPIRACY AGAINST JESUS

Matt. 26:1–5	**Mark 14:1–2**	**Luke 22:1–2**
¹ When Jesus had finished all these sayings, he said to his disciples, ²"You know that after two days the Passover is coming, and the Son of man will be delivered up to be crucified."	¹It was now two days before the Passover and the feast of Unleavened Bread.	¹Now the feast of Unleavened Bread drew near, which is called the Passover.
³Then the chief priests and the elders of the people gathered in the palace of the high priest, who was called Caiaphas, ⁴and took counsel together in order to arrest Jesus by stealth and kill him. ⁵But they said, "Not during the feast, lest there be a tumult among the people."	And the chief priests and the scribes were seeking how to arrest him by stealth, and kill him; ²for they said, "Not during the feast, lest there be a tumult of the people."	²And the chief priests and the scribes were seeking how to put him to death; for they feared the people.

This pericope is more than twice as long in Matthew's version than in the versions of Mark and Luke, but when we note what words are held in common by at least two of these texts, we find a curious phenomenon:

Words in Common	*Matt.*	*Mark*	*Luke*
now	O	X	X
two days	X	X	O
the Passover	X	X	X
the feast of Unleavened Bread	O	X	X
And	O	X	X
the chief priests and the	X	X	X
scribes were seeking how	O	X	X

to arrest	X	X	O
by stealth and kill	X	X	O
him	X	X	X
for	O	X	X
they said	X	X	O
Not during the feast, lest there be a tumult	X	X	O
the people	X	X	X

The peculiarity we note is that all of the words marked with an "X" above are found in Mark's Gospel. Furthermore, while Matthew and Mark sometimes agree with one another over against Luke (e.g., the words "to arrest") and while Mark and Luke sometimes agree with one another over against Matthew (e.g., "the feast of the Unleavened Bread"), we do not find Matthew and Luke agreeing with one another over against Mark. Obviously we have a literary relationship among these three texts, but can we define it more precisely?

There are two primary possibilities that come to the fore: either Matthew and Luke each copied their material from Mark (and did not make use of one another) or Mark is a collation of material drawn from Matthew and Luke. Both of these viewpoints are found in contemporary biblical scholarship.[6]

In the first instance, Mark is understood to be the earliest Gospel, because it gave rise to both Matthew and Luke. This relationship can be diagrammed as follows:

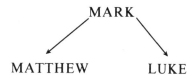

MARK

MATTHEW   LUKE

[6]A thorough discussion of various possibilities is to be found in Werner Georg Kümmel's *Introduction to the New Testament*. rev. ed., trans. Howard Clark Kee (Nashville and New York: Abingdon Press, 1975), pp. 38-80.

This view is the most common today among biblical scholars and is the necessary one if we are to speak at all of Q, as we will show later.

The other point of view holds that Mark is the last of the three Gospels to have been written. In the most popular statement of this position today,[7] the relationship of the Synoptic Gospels to one another can be diagrammed this way:

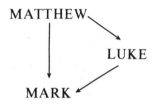

According to this view, Matthew was the first Gospel which was then used and modified by Luke. The last of the three to have been written was Mark who combined elements from both Matthew and Luke to come up with his Gospel.

There are other, far more complicated explanations of the relationship of these three Gospels to one another, but the two which we have given here suffice for our purposes and present the two leading hypotheses. But which of these two is the better solution to understanding the literary relations among these Gospels?

While both points of view have some problems, when all the texts that these three Gospels have in common are examined, most scholars accept the priority of Mark as the most satisfactory and hold that the view that Mark is the last Gospel is more difficult to defend. To name only a few of the problems associated with the view that Mark was the last of the Synoptic Gospels to have been written, we single out these: Mark is much shorter than Matthew and Luke; why did Mark leave out so much important material, like the

---

[7]William R. Farmer, *The Synoptic Problem. A Critical Analysis* (Dillsboro, NC: Western North Carolina Press, 1976).

infancy and resurrection narratives or the discourse material like Jesus' sermon on the mount (in Matthew) or the sermon on the plain (in Luke)? Why does Mark introduce errors into quotations from the Old Testament when both Matthew and Luke do not have these errors? But even more problematic is the notion that Mark would go through each sentence of Matthew and Luke and choose a phrase first from Matthew and then one from Luke within sentences where such picking and choosing appears to be entirely unimportant and arbitrary. These appear to be among the major objections to the hypothesis that Mark was the last of the Synoptics to have been written, but there are many other objections that can be raised.[8]

There are also some problems, however, with the hypothesis that Mark was the first Gospel to have been written, especially in the so-called "minor agreements" between Matthew and Luke over against Mark. Such minor agreements occur relatively frequently[9] but often in what seems insignificant phrases. Most of these are thought to be coincidental or accidental agreements that occurred when Matthew and Luke, independently of one another, refined some of Mark's less cultivated Greek. They may have simply used stereotypical expressions to correct or improve Mark's style. More complicated explanations of this, due to the manner of textual transmission of the biblical manuscripts, can also be given.[10]

[8]See the brief but clear compendium compiled by William A. Beardslee, *Literary Criticism of the New Testament*, in: *Guides to Biblical Scholarship. New Testament Series* (Philadelphia: Fortress Press, 1970), pp. 64–74.

[9]See Frans Neirynck, T. Hansen, and F. Van Segbroeck, *The Minor Agreements of Matthew and Luke against Mark with a Cumulative List*, in: *Bibliotheca Ephemeridum Theologicarum Lovaniensium*, 37 (Leuven: Leuven University Press, 1974), espec. pp. 49–195.

[10]Beardslee, p. 73, notes the complexity of the issue: "Some of these [agreements between Matthew and Luke against Mark] may be explained by independent, parallel editing of Mark by Matthew and by Luke, some by later assimilation of one text to the other. There was a strong tendency toward such assimilation in the process of copying; usually Matthew's form being the most familiar, was inserted into Luke and, for that matter, also into Mark in some cases. But it may also be the case that at times Matthew and Luke each drew independently on an oral tradition which was different than Mark."

When the arguments for and the objections against each of these leading positions are weighed, it seems that the priority of Mark has fewer problems than the other, and so we will proceed now to look at some further ramifications of the theory that understands Mark's Gospel to have been the first.

If we were to subtract from Matthew and Luke all the material that they borrowed from Mark, we would find three types of material remaining: some material that is found only in Matthew, which we designate as "M"; some material that is found only in Luke, which we designate as "L", and, finally, a very large amount of material that is common to both Matthew and Luke but which is missing in Mark. This material we designate as "Q."

The Q material is frequently very similar in wording and word order, as we note in the following pericope:

THE LAMENT OVER JERUSALEM

Matt. 23:37–39

Luke 13:34–35

[37]"O Jerusalem, Jerusalem, killing the prophets and stoning those who are sent to you! How often would I have gathered your children together as a hen gathers her brood under her wings, and you would not! [38]Behold, your house is forsaken and desolate. [39]For I tell you, you will not see me again, until you say, 'Blessed is he who comes in the name of the Lord.'"

[34]"O Jerusalem, Jerusalem, killing the prophets and stoning those who are sent to you! How often would I have gathered your children together as a hen gathers her brood under her wings, and you would not! [35]Behold, your house is forsaken! And I tell you, you will not see me until you say, 'Blessed is he who comes in the name of the Lord.'"

Such verbatim wording and word order requires a literary explanation. Indeed, when we survey the Q pericopes, we see that many of them are very similar both in the very nature of the material itself and in the precise wording. Most of the Q material consists of sayings of Jesus. Matthew and Luke sometimes preserve this material in the same order but place it in different parts of Mark's basic story line which both Matthew and Luke have followed. Since much of the

M and L material is also sayings, it may well be that some of this material was once part of Q also, but we have no certain way of proving that, since Q must be reconstructed from material that is found in both Matthew and Luke.[11] We can diagram the influence of these materials on Matthew and Luke in this way:

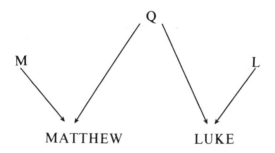

Thus Q, M and L are all sources for Matthew and Luke. When we add Mark to this, we have the complete literary sources for understanding the relation of the Synoptic Gospels to one another. The two primary sources are Mark and Q, and for this reason, this is called the "Two Source Hypothesis" but we also have the minor influences of the special M and L materials as well. The complete diagram explaining the Synoptic relations is as follows:

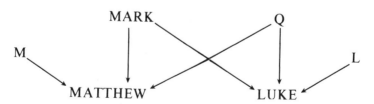

[11]Polag's reconstruction of Q does include special Lucan and special Matthaean material at points where the material coheres with that which certainly belongs to Q. It should be noted that M and L are probably not sources in and of themselves but may consist of individual oral traditions, some of which may have belonged to Q.

In a few instances, we find some traditions that are common to both Mark and Q. This has led some to suggest that Mark knew and borrowed from Q or vice versa, but it may only be a matter of common traditions which arrived in slightly different forms to Mark and Q.[12] To illustrate this issue we look at the pericope of the mustard seed parable:

THE PARABLE OF THE MUSTARD SEED

Matt. 13:31-32	Mark 4:30-32	Luke 13:18-19
[31]Another parable he put before them, saying, "The kingdom of heaven is like a grain of mustard seed which a man took and sowed in his field; [32]it is the smallest of all seeds, but when it has grown it	[30]And he said, "With what can we compare the kingdom of God, or what parable shall we use for it? [31]It is like a grain of mustard seed, which, when sown upon the ground, is the smallest of all the seeds on earth; [32]yet when it is sown it grows up and becomes the greatest of all shrubs, and puts forth large branches, so that the birds of the air can make nests in its shade."	[18]He said therefore, "What is the kingdom of God like? And to what shall I compare it? [19]It is like a grain of mustard seed which a man took and sowed in his garden;
is the greatest of shrubs and becomes a tree, so that the birds of the air come and make nests in its branches."		and it grew and became a tree, and the birds of the air made nests in its branches."

When we note down where the words common to these Gospels appear, we find a pattern that is not easy to interpret:

[12]The main arguments concerning the relationship of Q to Mark are clearly set forth by Rudolf Laufen, *Die Doppelüberlieferungen der Logienquelle und des Markusevangeliums*, in: *Bonner Biblische Beiträge*, 54 (Königstein/Ts.-Bonn: Verlag Peter Hanstein, 1980). Four primary theories are discussed: 1) the excerpt theory—Mark is dependent on Q in a direct literary sense, for Mark has taken excerpts from Q; 2) the reminiscence theory—Mark is dependent upon Q but this is not a direct literary dependence; rather, the Evangelist had seen Q and later repeats from memory or reminiscence some passages from Q; 3) Q as a developing entity—Q is both older and younger than Mark, since it was not yet a fixed entity, and Mark used an earlier level of Q than the version used by Matthew and Luke; 4) neither Mark knew Q nor Q knew Mark—the agreements between them go back to the same oral or written traditions which had been transmitted independently from one another. This last named theory is that of Laufen and is the most widely accepted view at present.

Words in Common	Matt.	Mark	Luke
he said	O	X	X
what	O	X	X
is like	X	X	X
the kingdom of	X	X	X
God	O	X	X
is like a grain of mustard seed which	X	X	X
a man took and sowed in his	X	O	X
is the smallest of all seeds	X	X	O
the greatest of shrubs	X	X	O
a tree	X	O	X
so that	X	X	O
the birds of the air	X	X	X
make	X	X	O
nest in its	X	X	X
branches	X	O	X

In this case, we find Matthew and Luke sometimes agreeing with one another over against Mark, especially noteworthy in the words "a tree" and "branches" and also in the phrase "a man took and sowed in his." These verbatim examples could not be coincidental but represent a different version of the mustard seed parable from the version we find in Mark. Both Matthew and Luke had two versions of this parable before them, one from Mark which spoke of the shrub image, the other from Q which spoke of the tree and branches image. Matthew combined this material together in a way different from Luke. The mustard seed parable, therefore, is one of those few passages that was found, though in a different form, in both of the earliest gospel sources, namely Mark and Q.

In summary, Q is one of the two primary sources for the Gospels of Matthew and Luke and in a few instances has material that is found in a different form in Mark. Q no longer exists as a separate text like that which once lay before Matthew and Luke as they composed their Gospels, but its contents can now be tentatively reconstructed from

Matthew and Luke by subtracting the Marcan material and studying the remaining material that is common to both. Care must be taken, however, even in the subtraction of the Marcan material, as the mustard seed parable indicates. Each text needs to be carefully examined.

The Letter Designation "Q"

How and why the hypothetical sayings source that we now call "Q" came to be named by this particular letter of the alphabet is not really known with certainty. The most frequently repeated explanation is that Q is merely an abbreviation for the German word *Quelle* which means "source." This may, in fact, be correct, but there is also the possibility that the use of this letter designation was purely arbitrary much as mathematicians arbitrarily assign the letters "X", "Y" and "Z" to certain quantities.

It should be noted, however, that the claim of the English scholar, J. Armitage Robinson, to have been the first to use the symbol "Q" for the sayings source has not been supported by the evidence of his printed works; rather, the symbol is to be traced back almost certainly to German scholars.[13] As early as 1876 Julius Wellhausen was using "Q" (from the Latin word *quattuor*) as a designation for a foundational document (*Vierbundesbuch*) in the Old Testament. A young group of theologians at Göttingen, among whom were Johannes Weiss, Wilhelm Bousset and Paul Wernle, who were undoubtedly familiar with Wellhausen's work, may have picked up using the Q symbol from him and began to use it either consciously or unconsciously for a similar kind of situation in the New Testament.[14]

In any case, Johannes Weiss appears to have been the first to have used "Q" to designate the New Testament sayings

[13]W.F. Howard, "The Origin of the Symbol 'Q,'" *The Expository Times*, 50 (1938–1939), 379–380.

[14]This is the conjecture of Lou H. Silbermann, "Whence *Siglum* Q? A Conjecture," *Journal of Biblical Literature*, 98 (1979), 287–288.

source. In an essay in 1890,[15] he refers to the verses of Luke
11:14-26 as coming partly "from the sayings source (*Redenquelle*), which is to be reconstructed from Matthew and
Luke (Q) ... " After this passage, he uses the symbol Q
without brackets and without further explanation. In this
case "Q" was used to designate "*Redenquelle*," the sayings
source. Why Weiss used "Q" instead of "R" for "*Redenquelle*" remains a mystery, but it seems likely that the Q
designation became the recognized symbol for the sayings
through the writings of Weiss.[16]

Other designations are still to be found, as well. Sometimes this "document" is also referred to as the *logia* (=
sayings), the "sayings source", or "sayings collection." "Q"
remains, however, the most common designation for this
material.

Genre and Oral Nature of Q

While the letter designation "Q" for the sayings source is a
modern name for this material, the term "sayings" to refer to
a collection, such as we have in Q, is an ancient term.[17] In

[15]Johannes Weiss, "Die Verteidigung Jesu gegen den Vorwurf des Bündnisses
mit Beelzebul," *Theologische Studien und Kritiken*, 63 (1890), 555-569, espec.
557.

[16]See both Harvey K. McArthur, "The Origin of the 'Q' Symbol," *The Expository Times*, 88 (1977), 119-120 and Frans Neirynck, "The Symbol Q (= Quelle),"
Ephemerides Theologicae Lovanienses, 54 (1978), 119-125.

[17]See James M. Robinson's important essay, "LOGOI SOPHON. On the *Gat-
tung* of Q," *Trajectories through Early Christianity*, ed. James M. Robinson and
Helmut Koester (Philadelphia: Fortress Press, 1971), pp. 71-113. I have borrowed his references to Acts 20:35 and the Gospel of Thomas, but he cites several
other examples. In the latter part of his essay (pp. 103-113), Robinson defines the
genre of sayings collections, including that of Q, more precisely as "sayings of the
sages" or "sayings of the wise," because he finds the genre developing out of a
Jewish wisdom tradition. But in his study on Christian prophecy in the Synoptics, M. Eugene Boring, *Sayings of the Risen Jesus*, in: *Society for New Testament Studies, Monograph Series*, 46 (Cambridge: Cambridge University Press,
1982), pp. 180-181, asks whether "sayings of the wise" best describes Q, for Q is
not a Christian Book of Proverbs, despite its contact with the wisdom tradition in
both form and content. The Q community lived by revelation rather than by
traditional wisdom. The animating factor in Q was the present/future mode of
prophecy.

Acts 20:35, a book written by the same author as the Gospel of Luke, we find a formula that speaks of "sayings of the Lord" that is followed by the quotation of one such saying of Jesus:

> In all things I have shown you that by so toiling one must help the weak, remembering the *sayings*[18] of the Lord, how he said, "It is more blessed to give than to receive."
>
> Acts 20:35

The Evangelist Luke, therefore, knew of a literary genre called "sayings," and this designation for a collection is confirmed by the beginning of the Gospel of Thomas, which is a collection of Jesus sayings that is in some ways quite similar to Q:

> These are the secret *sayings* which the living Jesus spoke and which Didymos Judas Thomas wrote down.[19]

It is proper, therefore, to speak of Q as a *sayings* source, since not only is the content one of sayings but it is the designation used by the ancients themselves for such a collection as Q.

It is a curious fact, however, that sayings traditions associated with Jesus, including those in Q, were not always greeted with great enthusiasm in the churches represented by the various New Testament writings. The Apostle Paul, for instance, cites only a few "sayings of the Lord" and maintains a generally defensive position over against the sayings tradition.[20] Likewise, when one realizes that the

---

[18]I have changed the RSV rendering of "words" to read "sayings," since the latter rather than the former captures the sense of the passage, for "sayings" rather than individual "words" are meant. See Robinson, pp. 96–97.

[19]Cameron, p. 25.

[20]For a discussion of the "sayings of the Lord," see David Dungan, *The Sayings of Jesus in the Churches of Paul* (Philadelphia: Fortress Press, 1971). Werner H. Kelber, *The Oral and the Written Gospel. The Hermeneutics of Speaking and Writing in the Synoptic Tradition, Mark, Paul and Q* (Philadelphia: Fortress Press, 1983), pp. 198–199, discusses why Paul was defensive in regard to the sayings of Jesus tradition.

Evangelist Mark is relating the ministry of Jesus together with material about his suffering and death, the relatively few sayings of Jesus used by him seem odd, and even though Matthew and Luke used the sayings of Q in the composition of their own Gospels, they did so at the expense of Q's integrity as a theological writing in its own right. In a certain sense, we may say that these two evangelists have "decontextualized"[21] Q in the composition of their Gospels. In fact, we find a happy home for such sayings only in Gnosticism, a philosophical-religious movement that was treated with a great deal of reserve and later by denunciation by the larger church. It is also in Gnostic circles that we find the sayings collection of the Gospel of Thomas, which we noted already above.

But why was the sayings genre treated so circumspectly by the writers of the New Testament? An answer may lie in the very nature of the sayings genre itself, which is closely related to oral transmission of the material it contains. The proclaimers of such materials were prophets in their communities and these proclaimers of Jesus' sayings identified themselves so completely with him that they claimed to speak in his name, thereby creating new sayings of Jesus that certainly did not go back to his historical person. These prophets could do this in good faith for they believed that there was a continuity between themselves and the Jesus who was still alive and speaking through them. In the case of Q and of other collections of Jesus' sayings, the prophets were not bound to the historical Jesus of the past but had a much more dynamic perspective. They understood Jesus still to be speaking through them. They had no thought at all of distinguishing between the pre-Easter and post-Easter Jesus because for these prophets the earthly Jesus and the risen Jesus were one and the same. The sayings genre was a unique means of continuing the present authority of Jesus.[22] As such, however, there were few controls on what might be

---

[21]I have borrowed this word from Kelber, p. 200, and have relied on his discussion, pp. 199–200.

[22]Kelber, pp. 200–202.

set forth as genuine teaching of Jesus and there was the ever present danger of departing radically from the historical grounding and ending in esoteric thought.

By incorporating the Q material into their Gospels, Matthew and Luke eliminated the problem just stated. The writing down of the sayings into their Gospels put an effective end to the dynamic principle that motivated the Q prophets, and the theology of Q as a document in its own right was destroyed as its materials were subsumed into a different theological context, especially one that treated the meaning of Jesus' death—something entirely missing in Q.[23]

The fact that Q has no passion narrative relating the final suffering and death of Jesus marks a radical departure from the biblical Gospels' portrayal of Jesus. Not even the death of Jesus is spoken of in Q,[24] simply because there was no need to speak of it. Q's theological interests lay in Jesus' preaching and in his role in manifesting the kingdom of God in his present life and future coming. (See the section on *The Kingdom of God* below.) The emphasis on these features of Jesus' ministry and person virtually precludes discussion of his death, for as Werner Kelber points out, "A tradition that focuses on the continuation of Jesus' words cannot simultaneously bring to consciousness what put an end to his speaking."[25]

An examination of the form of the materials in Q[26] shows how close they are to oral transmission; even the few narra-

---

[23]Kelber, p. 207, states, "The written gospel first appeared in the history of the tradition by elevating the earthly Jesus at the price of silencing the living Lord;" cf. further pp. 206–208.

[24]Q knew of the death of Jesus, of course, but chose not to discuss it or its significance. Only in Q 58 do we find a reference to the cross:

> And whoever does not take up one's cross
>   and come after me,
> cannot be my disciple.
>   Q 58 lines 5–7

Otherwise, the death of Jesus can only be surmised from the sayings which speak of "killing the prophets;" cf. Q 36 lines 28–33; Q 51 lines 1–3.

[25]Kelber, p. 201.

[26]For the discussion of forms, I have drawn upon the classic definitions of Rudolf Bultmann, *The History of the Synoptic Tradition*. rev. ed., trans. John

tives of Q betray a greater interest in the dialogue which is usually a part of them than in the story per se. For instance, in the controversy story of Q 29 we have a narrative of an event that describes an exorcism and a dispute over how this casting out of a demon was accomplished, but the focus of interest and the bulk of the material lie in the dialogue between the disputants:

> And he was casting out a demon,
> and it was dumb.
> And when the demon had gone out, the person
>   who was dumb spoke,
> and the people marveled.
> But some of them said,
> "By Beelzebul, the prince of demons,
> he casts out demons."
> But knowing their thoughts, he said to them,

> "Every kingdom divided against itself is laid waste,
>   and every house divided against itself will not stand.
> And if Satan is divided against himself,
>   how will his kingdom stand?

> And if I cast out demons by Beelzebul
>   by whom do your children cast them out?
>   Therefore they shall be your judges.
> But if it is by the finger of God that I cast out demons,
>   then the kingdom of God has come upon you."

Q 29

Likewise, in the miracle story of the healing of the centurion's servant, the emphasis falls not on the healing but upon Jesus' discussion with the centurion and Jesus' very positive evaluation of the centurion's faith:

Marsh (New York and Evanston: Harper & Row, Publishers, 1968). Howard Clark Kee, *Jesus in History. An Approach to the Study of the Gospels.* 2nd ed. (New York: Harcourt Brace Jovanovich, Inc., 1977), pp. 84–87, has assigned each passage of Q to a specific form but has used a different categorization of forms.

And when Jesus finished
these sayings,
he entered Capernaum.

And a centurion [came forward to him beseeching,
"Lord, my servant is lying at home
paralyzed, in terrible distress."
And he said to him, "I will come and heal him."
And the centurion answered him and said,][27]
"Lord, I am not worthy
to have you come under my roof;
but say the word, and my servant will be healed.
For I am a man under authority
with soldiers under me,
and I say to one, 'Go' and he goes,
and to another, 'Come,' and he comes,
and to my slave, 'Do this,' and he does it."
When Jesus heard him, he marveled
and said to those who followed him,
"[Truly], I say to you,
not even in Israel have I found such faith."
[And his servant was healed at that very moment.]

Q 13

Even the cult legend of Jesus' baptism, which is primarily a
narrative, ends with a heavenly voice declaring who Jesus is.
What this voice says is the punchline, so to speak, of the
story and the place where attention is focused:

[And Jesus came to John
to be baptized by him,
and when Jesus had been baptized, the heaven was
opened
and the Spirit descended upon him as a dove,

---

[27]For an explanation of the use of brackets (and other symbols) within the
quotations of the Q sayings, see pp. 112-114.

> and a voice from heaven came,
> "You are my Son;
> today I have begotten you."]

Q 3

If we compare the pure legend form of the temptation story in Mark's Gospel with that of Q's version, we see immediately the striking difference between them. Mark's narrative is very short, a story without dialogue:

> The Spirit immediately drove him out into the wilderness. And he was in the wilderness forty days, tempted by Satan; and he was with the wild beasts; and the angels ministered to him.

Mark 1:12-13

This contrasts with the much lengthier account in Q which is more interested in the dialogue between Jesus and the devil:

> And Jesus was led up by the Spirit in the wilderness
> to be tempted by the devil,
> and he ate nothing for forty days,
> and afterward he was hungry.
>
> And the devil said to him,
> "If you are the Son of God,
> command this stone to become bread."
> And Jesus answered,
> "It is written,
> 'You shall not live by bread alone.' "
>
> And the devil took him to Jerusalem
> and set him on the pinnacle of the temple,
> and said to him,
> "If you are the Son of God,
> throw yourself down;
> for it is written,
> 'He will give his angels charge of you,'
> and 'On their hands they will bear you up

lest you strike your foot against a stone.' "

And Jesus answered him,
"Again it is written,
'You shall not tempt the Lord your God.' "

And the devil took him to a very high mountain
and showed him all the kingdoms of the world
and the glory of them,
and he said to him,
"All these I will give you, if you will worship me."
And Jesus answered him,
"It is written,
'You shall worship the Lord your God,
and him only shall you serve.' "

Then the devil left him.

Q 4

Thus in almost all cases in Q, the narrative portions only serve to highlight a saying or dialogue or merely to introduce sayings materials.

The Q sayings that are devoid of narrative include virtually all the forms that we find elsewhere in the Synoptic tradition. In Q we find good examples of each kind of sayings material. Just a few of them are presented here to acquaint the reader with the riches of the forms in the Q document, all of which stem from the oral tradition.

Among the parabolic forms we find such simple comparisons as Q 36 lines 2–3:

For you cleanse the outside of the cup and of the plate,
but the inside is full of extortion and rapacity.

and the slightly longer comparison of Q 38 lines 8–12:

Are not five sparrows sold for two pennies?
And not one of them will fall to the ground without God's
will.
But even the hairs of your head are all numbered.

Fear not;
you are of more value than many sparrows.

With the vignette of the searching out of the lost sheep, the comparison approaches a story:

What man of you, having a hundred sheep,
if he has lost one of them,
does not leave the ninety-nine in the wilderness
and go in search of the one which is lost, until he finds
it?
And when he has found it, he lays it on his shoulders,
rejoicing.
And when he comes home,
he calls together his friends and his neighbors,
saying to them, "Rejoice with me,"
for I have found my sheep which was lost.

Q 61 lines 1–9

Such a lengthy vignette is not often found in Q, but another example is the familiar parable of the mustard seed (Q 52). In Q there are no extended, lengthy parable stories (known as "example stories") such as the parables of the good Samaritan (Luke 10:29-37) or the prodigal son (Luke 15:11-32).

The bulk of sayings in Q is aphoristic, and these aphorisms take several forms.[28] One of the important aphoristic forms in Q is that of proverbs or words of wisdom, which are conclusions based on experiences.[29] There are a number of short wise sayings like this example:

---

[28]A thorough discussion of aphorisms that takes note of Q materials is that of John Dominic Crossan, *In Fragments. The Aphorisms of Jesus* (San Francisco: Harper & Row, Publishers, 1983).

[29]See the detailed listing of proverbs and related forms in Q in both Richard A. Edwards, *A Theology of Q. Eschatology, Prophecy, and Wisdom* (Philadelphia: Fortress Press, 1976), pp. 49, 58–79 and Charles E. Carlston, "Wisdom and Eschatology in Q," in: *Logia. Les paroles de Jésus—The Sayings of Jesus*, in: *Bibliotheca Ephemeridum Theologicarum Lovaniensium*, 59 (Leuven: Leuven University, 1982), 108-111.

The disciple is not above the teacher:
   [it is enough for the disciple
     to be like the teacher.]

Q 9 lines 3–5

Other sayings similar to proverbs also bear prophetic qualities, like beatitudes. Sayings such as the following passage can be placed in either a proverbial or prophetic category:

Blessed are you when (people) hate you
   and exclude and revile you
   and utter evil against you
   on account of the son of man.

Q 5 lines 10–13

Prophetic/apocalyptic sayings abound in Q and are revelatory in nature. They proclaim and announce,[30] like the example:

I tell you,
   in that night there will be two men in one bed;
     one that will be taken and one left.
   There will be two women grinding at the mill;
     one will be taken and one left.

Q 73

Judgments and warnings also belong to this category of sayings:

If they say to you,
   "Lo, he is in the wilderness,"
do not go out;
   "Lo, he is in the inner rooms,"
do not believe it.

---

[30]See Edwards, pp. 44–57, espec. pp. 49–57 for a listing of Q prophetic passages. A more technical discussion on prophetic forms in Q is found in Boring, pp. 137–182.

> For as lightening comes from the east
>   and shines as far as the west,
> so will the son of man be in his day.

Q 69 lines 1–8

Yet another category of sayings deals with law and community rules, which, in turn, reflect the goals and practices of the community that proclaims them. The famous divorce saying is a prime example of a law saying:

> Every one who divorces his wife (and marries another)
>   commits adultery,
> and whoever marries a divorced woman
>   commits adultery.

Q 64

and the saying about to whom and how often one should forgive is another example of a community rule:

> If your friend sins, give a rebuke,
>   and if the friend repents, grant forgiveness;
> and if the friend sins against you seven times in the day
>   and turns seven times, and says, "I repent,"
>   you must forgive that one.

Q 67

The last Bultmannian category of sayings is the "I" sayings. They are easy to identify because they use the first person pronoun "I," but as a category it is not very useful since many "I" sayings fit other categories as well. One simple example is Q 19:

> Go your way; behold, I send you out
>   as lambs in the midst of wolves.

This passage is an "I" saying, but it is also a prophetic saying that makes a pronouncement and at the same time employs a parabolic comparison.

What all these sayings have in common is their orality.[31]
They are words that have been spoken and still maintain the
quality of speakability. Even though they have been written
down, they have for the most part preserved the oral character of their origin. Individual sayings do not yet reflect the
interconnections between Jesus' preaching and his role, for
that can only first be seen when the Q document is taken as a
whole.

One of the pressing problems in the reconstruction of Q
from Matthew and Luke is that it is presumed that the text
of Q that lay before each evangelist was the same. Indeed,
there are a number of individual sayings that are nearly
verbatim the same in Matthew and Luke, as we noted in "the
lament over Jerusalem" in Q 51, and that might lead one to
conclude that the same Q text was used by Matthew and
Luke. This may be an oversimplified explanation, however,
for many parallel sayings also depart from one another in
more than just a few words, as this example shows which
begins with the same wording but varies considerably in the
latter parts:

GOD'S ANSWERING OF PRAYER

Matt. 7:7-11

[7]"Ask, and it will
be given you; seek, and you will find;
knock, and it will be opened to you.
[8]For every one who asks receives,
and he who seeks finds, and to him
who knocks it will be opened. [9]Or
what man of you, if his son asks him
for bread, will give him a stone?
[10]Or if he asks for a fish, will give
him a serpent?

[11]If
you then, who are evil, know how to
give good gifts to your children, how
much more will your Father who is in
heaven give good things to those who
ask him!

Luke 11:9-13

[9]And I tell you,"Ask, and it will
be given you; seek, and you will find;
knock, and it will be opened to you.
[10]For every one who asks receives,
and he who seeks finds, and to him
who knocks it will be opened.
[11]What father among you, if his son
asks for
a fish, will instead of a fish give
him a serpent; [12]or if he asks for an
egg, will give him a scorpion? [13]If
you then, who are evil, know how to
give good gifts to your children, how
much more will the heavenly Father
give the holy Spirit to those who ask
him!"

[31]In this and the following paragraph, I have drawn upon the work of Kelber,
p. 23.

While this could be due to the different redactional work of
Matthew and Luke on the same Q text, it could also be due
to a difference in the text of Q that was available to each,
because the very oral nature of Q may have resisted fixed
wording in every case. Thus the following diagram[32] represents a more complicated line of transmission from the Q
document at some earlier stage till its incorporation into
Matthew and Luke:

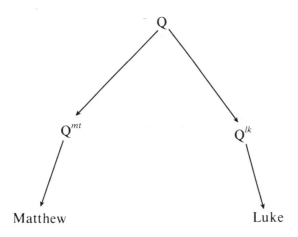

If this diagram accurately reflects the transmission of Q to
Matthew and Luke, all reconstructions of the precise wording of Q are doomed to failure. But even in this case, a fairly
accurate sense of the document can be arrived at and in
some instances even the precise wording of certain sayings.
Most who have attempted reconstructions of Q have maintained the simpler theory that the text of Q before Matthew
and Luke was essentially the same.

---

[32]This diagram is suggested by Dieter Zeller, *Kommentar zur Logienquelle,* in:
Stuttgarter Kleiner Kommentar, Neues Testament, 21 (Stuttgart: Verlag Katholisches Bibelwerk, 1984), p. 18, to demonstrate the view, held by some, that
Matthew and Luke had before them versions of Q that were different from one
another. The symbols Q^{mt} and Q^{lk} represent these two different recensions.

Date and Place of Composition of Q

One of the difficulties in assigning a date to the Q document is the fact that its traditions and the document itself went through various phases of development and redaction. At what point, then, can we speak of the document Q?

Normally we do not speak of Christian communities until after the resurrection of Jesus, when the original circle of disciples gathered together once again, following their dispersal at the death of Jesus and after his appearances to them following his resurrection, but with the beginnings of the Q community a very different sort of situation may have occurred, because the death and resurrection of Jesus were not at the core of Q thought.

The beginnings of the Q community are to be found in the historical ministry of Jesus with his call to repentance and acceptance of the kingdom of God.[33] The disciples of Jesus, but not necessarily members of the Twelve,[34] continued to preach his message and so continued to transmit his sayings, perhaps in complete ignorance of the events that surrounded the death of Jesus in Jerusalem. In other words, the rationale for preserving and transmitting Jesus' sayings existed *before* his death.

The resurrection of Jesus, of course, had its effect on those who were already continuing his preaching, and this gave rise to still more sayings, especially those which spoke of Jesus' coming as an apocalyptic figure at the end time, but there is no reason to place the beginnings of the Q community in the post-Easter period; rather, the charismatic itinerant prophets whose materials make up the core of the Q document may have themselves formed the only group of

---

[33]See the important essay of Heinz Schürmann, "Die vorösterlichen Anfänge der Logientradition. Versuch eines formgeschichtlichen Zugangs zum Leben Jesu," in: *Der historische Jesus und der kerygmatische Christus*, ed. H. Ristow and K. Matthiae. 3rd ed. (Berlin: Evangelische Verlagsanstalt, 1964), pp. 193-210 and the additional comments of Athanasius Polag, *Die Christologie der Logienquelle*, in: *Wissenschaftliche Monographien zum Alten und Neuen Testament*, 45 (Neukirchen-Vluyn: Neukirchner Verlag, 1977), pp. 192-197.

[34]No names of the disciples of Jesus appear in Q.

people that maintained an unbroken connection with the historical Jesus.

Even though the disciples of Jesus are sent by him to all the towns of Israel (cf. Q 18 line 2; Q 20; Q 42), the biblical Gospels place the bulk of Jesus' ministry in northern Galilee, where we might expect the founders of Q theology also to have had their primary locus. The present form of Q indicates that that may indeed be the case, for even though Q does mention Jerusalem twice (Q 4 line 11; Q 51 line 1) and the region around the Jordan once (Q 1 line 7), the other places cited are either in northern Galilee or in western Syria. The naming of the towns of Chorazin and Bethsaida (Q 22 lines 1–2) is particularly significant, because these towns play no role elsewhere in the Synoptic tradition and their mention in passing suggests familiarity with the area and, perhaps, the places from which these materials came.[35] Capernaum, likewise, belongs to this area and is named twice in Q (13 line 3; 22 line 8). The Gentile cities of Tyre and Sidon, cities of western Syria, are named in Q 22 line 7, and their geographical location is not far from northern Galilee.

That northern Galilee and western Syria are the area in which the Q community was centered is supported by a look at early Christian literature produced in Syria. The writing known as the *Didache* (or *The Teaching of the Twelve Apostles*) certainly came from Syria and bears a number of similarities to the Synoptic Gospel of Matthew,[36] which suggests that they may have come from the same geographical area. This is confirmed by a study of other extra-biblical writings that center on the person of Peter,[37] for these writings were concentrated in Syria, whose leading city,

[35]So Jack Dean Kingsbury, *Jesus Christ in Matthew, Mark and Luke*, in: *Proclamation Commentaries* (Philadelphia: Fortress Press, 1981), p. 24.

[36]See Helmut Koester, "GNOMAI DIAPHOROI. The Origin and Nature of Diversification in the History of Early Christianity," in: *Trajectories through Early Christianity*, ed. James M. Robinson and Helmut Koester (Philadelphia: Fortress Press, 1971), p. 124.

[37]Koester, p. 125, cites seveal examples of "Petrine" literature from western Syrian provenance.

Antioch, claimed Peter as one of its bishops. The Gospel of Matthew, being the oldest of such Peter traditions, is to be located in western Syria as well. This is significant, because Matthew is one of the two sources that preserves the contents of Q. It would be easy to understand how Matthew knew of Q, if the community was located primarily in northern Galilee and western Syria.

The location of the place where Luke's Gospel was composed is notoriously difficult to pinpoint, but the large amount of Antiochian material used by Luke in the Book of Acts may suggest some connection of that author with the city of Antioch.[38] Perhaps it was here that Luke obtained the Q material he was to use in the composition of his Gospel. (See more below.)

Yet another reason for suspecting some connection of Q material with northern Galilee and western Syria is the existence of another sayings source, the Gospel of Thomas, which belongs to the eastern Syrian traditions surrounding the person of Thomas.[39] Although it remains a question whether or not the Gospel of Thomas is a development from Q in one of its forms, it certainly consists of smaller collections of sayings, some of which are also to be found in Q.[40] Some of the sayings in special Luke, the material peculiar to

[38]The earliest external evidence for the authorship of Luke's Gospel is the so-called Anti-Marcionite prologue, which begins: "Luke is a Syrian of Antioch, a doctor by profession, who was a disciple of the apostles, and later followed Paul until his martyrdom." This same prologue says later of Luke that "impelled by the Holy Spirit [he] wrote this whole Gospel in the regions of Achaea;" see text in Reginald H. Fuller, *A Critical Introduction to the New Testament*, in: *Studies in Theology*, corrected ed. (London: Duckworth, 1971), p. 121. What is of special interest to us is the ascription of this Gospel to an evangelist from Syria, despite the claim that the Gospel itself was written elsewhere.

[39]Koester, pp. 127–136.

[40]So Helmut Koester, "One Jesus and Four Primitive Gospels," in: *Trajectories through Early Christianity*, ed. James M. Robinson and Helmut Koester (Philadelphia: Fortress Press, 1971), p. 186. In the essay cited in our footnote no. 36, written three years earlier than this one, Koester had a different view, p. 135: "We are here not advocating the specific synoptic source Q as the literary source for the Gospel of Thomas, since the basis of Thomas is certainly not identical with any possible form of the second source common to Matthew and Luke." Cf. also the less technical but balanced discussion of this issue by Shawn Carruth, "Ears to Hear," *The Bible Today*, 21 (March 1983), 89–95.

Luke which we have designated by the letter "L," are parallel to sayings in the Gospel of Thomas but are not found in Q or Matthew. The presence of this sayings material in the Gospel of Luke again suggests a Syrian connection with the Gospel. The Lucan writings betray, then, both eastern and western Syrian influence, making it quite possible that Q was known from the western Syrian materials taken up by the author.

While we can locate the center of Q influence in northern Galilee and western Syria, it is more difficult to situate the place of the writing down of the material in Q. Undoubtedly, the first sayings were to be found in Aramaic, but in its present reconstructed form Q is a Greek writing, even citing biblical references primarily from the Septuagint, the Greek version of the Old Testament. Since Aramaic was spoken by some in Syria, and Greek was spoken by some in northern Galilee, we have no certainty in assigning the specific place of Greek composition or of any of its various redactions, but the final redaction was known to both Matthew and Luke in western Syria.

The date of Q is also difficult to determine. Certainly it predated Matthew and Luke, but because nothing is said about the destruction of Jerusalem in 70 C.E., we can assume that it predates that event and, therefore, also predates the Gospel of Mark, since Mark was probably written either during the Jewish War (66-70 C.E.) or shortly after it. Q therefore had its beginnings with the ministry of the historical Jesus and was completed as a document in the form we know it sometime before the year 70 C.E.

God in Q

It seems fitting that we begin our look at the key elements of Q theology with the proper concern of theology—which is God. The word "theology" means literally the "study of God," and Q provides us with numerous glimpses into its understanding of who God is and what this divine being is like.

The God of the Q document is the God of the Jews who first formed and joined the Jesus movement, at least, in one of its strands. The earliest Christians were in fact Christian-Jews and, as such, shared most of the same understandings about God that other Jews had in the middle of the first century C.E. Except, perhaps, for the very latest stages of Q tradition, the composition of the Q community consisted entirely of Christian-Jews (See the section entitled "The Q Community and Its Mission.") and it maintained the validity of Jewish law, the Torah, preserving a saying of Jesus that underscores that fact:

> Truly, I say to you,
> till heaven and earth pass away,
>   not a dot will pass away from the law.

Q 63

In this very Jewish milieu of Q, we have a single God, who is named in three different ways, namely, as "God," as "Father," and as "Lord." These are the ways that the God of the Jews is also spoken of in the Old Testament, which was also the sacred scriptures for the Q community. It should be noted from the outset that in Q, Jesus is never called "God" or "Father," and there is no confusion of the identities of the two with one another, though some lack of clarity surrounds the "Lord" designation which was also used for Jesus. (See the subsection entitled "Jesus as Lord.")

This God is described in Q as the "Lord of heaven and earth" (Q 24 line 4), as the one who reigns over all creation, including his angels (Q 4 lines 17–18; Q 39). His dwelling place is in heaven; therefore, the voice of the Father speaks from heaven at Jesus' baptism:

> And a voice from heaven came,
> "You are my Son;
> today I have begotten you."

Q 3 lines 5–7

Yet the Father's presence in heaven is not a hindrance to his awareness of the needs of his earthly creatures and his ability to meet those needs in his ongoing creative activity:

> Therefore I tell you,
> do not be anxious about your life, what you shall eat,
>   nor about your body, what you shall put on.
> Is not life more than food,
>   and the body more than clothing?
>
> Look at the ravens,
>   they neither sow nor reap
>   nor gather into barns,
> and yet God feeds them.
> Of how much more value are you than the birds!
>
> And which of you by being anxious
>   can add a cubit to your span of life?
> And why are you anxious about clothing?
>
> Consider the lilies, how they grow;
>   they neither toil nor spin.
> Yet I tell you,
> that not even Solomon in all his glory
>   was arrayed like one of these.
> But if the grass which is alive in the field today,
>   and tomorrow is thrown into the oven,
>   is so clothed by God,
> how much more will he clothe you, who are of little faith?
>
> And do not be anxious saying,
>   "What shall we eat?" or "What shall we drink?" or "What
>   shall we wear?"
>   For the Gentiles seek all these things;
> and your Father knows that you need them.
> But seek first his kingdom,
>   and these things shall be yours as well.

Q 43 lines 1–28

God's control over creation and concern for it is so complete
that not a sparrow will fall to the ground without his will,
and even the hairs of people's heads are all numbered by
him:

> Are not five sparrows sold for two pennies?
> And not one of them will fall to the ground without God's
>   will.
> But even the hairs of your head are all numbered.
>   Fear not;
>   you are of more value than many sparrows.

Q 38 lines 8–12

The last line of the preceding quotation underscores a
peculiarity of God: he has a special concern for humankind
which is manifest in several ways. He has chosen to reveal
himself and his will through his law and the holy scriptures
(Q 63; Q 4) and even sent his Wisdom and Spirit among
humans, expecially through prophets (Q 36 lines 27–35; Q 3
line 4; Q 41; Q 15). In his mercy (Q 7 lines 1–2), love and
justice (Q 36 line 10), God wishes the salvation of humanity,
to free people from the power of the devil so that they may
have a share in his everlasting reign. (See the section entitled
"The Kingdom of God.")

As a concerned Father, he listens to the prayers of his
children:

> If you then, who are evil,
>   know how to give gifts to your children,
> how much more will the heavenly Father
>   give good things to those who ask him.

Q 28 lines 6–9

His children turn to him for all their needs, calling on the
Father:

When you pray, say:
Father,
hallowed be thy name.
    Thy kingdom come.
Give us this day our daily bread.
And forgive us our debts,
    as we also have forgiven our debtors;
and lead us not into temptation.

Q 26

The attitude of people before their creator is one of worship and of service to him alone (Q 4), because divided loyalties are not possible:

No one can serve two masters;
    for either you will hate the one and love the other,
    or will be devoted to the one and despise the other.
You cannot serve God and mammon.

Q 65

That humankind has failed in serving God is quite often referred to in Q by its call to repentance and by its threat of judgment. God rejoices over the repentant sinners (Q 61) but in his justice condemns those who reject him and refuse to repent:

But you will be thrown into the outer darkness.
There people will weep and gnash their teeth.

Q 55 lines 5–6

The new insight about God that the Q community proclaims is how he has worked through and continues to work through the person of Jesus, who will also take over the task of judgment at the end time. This Jesus is Son of God in a unique way. How this is understood by the Q community is treated below under the section entitled "The Person and Role of Jesus in Q." The God of Q is not, then, a "new" God but a God who has revealed himself and his reign in a new way, namely, through Jesus.

The Kingdom of God

The dominant theological concern of the Q document is the proclamation of the kingdom of God. The term "kingdom of God" refers to God's sovereignty or reign at the end time, when Satan's control over the kingdoms of the world is overcome forever. Q speaks of the kingdom of God in a twofold manner, for it claims on the one hand that God's reign was already present and manifest in Jesus' life and ministry, and on the other hand, that the kingdom's advent is still a future event associated with God's judgment at the end of time. Both of these ways of speaking of God's reign are treated in some depth by Q, so we will look more closely at each of them.

PRESENCE OF THE KINGDOM

Certainly the more startling of these two ways of looking at the kingdom of God is the one which sees it as already present in Jesus' ministry. It is present in the sense that God's decisive reign has begun to break in with the words and deeds of his prophetic Son, Jesus. In common theological parlance, this is called "realized" or "present eschatology," for the end time is already present, at least, in an initial way.

This is most clearly seen in a passage where even Jesus' detractors admit that he performs exorcisms. A dispute arose, however, concerning the means by which he casts out demons (Q 29). According to some, he did this by Beelzebul, the prince of demons, but Jesus argues that that would make no sense, because Satan would then be working against himself. Instead, Jesus offers a different explanation for his wondrous actions, saying, "But if it is by the finger of God that I cast out demons, then the kingdom of God has come upon you" (Q 29 lines 16–17).

The implications of these few words are enormous, for Jesus is claiming that the exorcisms which he performs are themselves manifestations of the kingdom of God already present. In other words, the end time has begun, and Jesus' ministry shows forth the presence of God's reign.[41] The Q community, no doubt, understood the other wondrous deeds of Jesus to also indicate that presence, so that Jesus' response to John the Baptist must be seen in this context as well:

> Go and tell John what you see and hear:
>> the blind receive their sight and the lame walk,
>> lepers are cleansed and the deaf hear,
>> the dead are raised up, and the poor have good news
>>> preached to them ...

Q 14 lines 6–9

These words are borrowed, in part, from the prophet Isaiah's vision of the messianic age, when God's sovereignty would reign supreme. (See Appendix IV for the Septuagint passages related to Q 14.) These words of scripture were chosen to indicate that this glorious end time has already begun in the ministry of Jesus.

The fact of the presence of the kingdom is underscored once again in the cryptic words of Q 62:

> The law and the prophets were until John;
> since then the kingdom of God has suffered violence,
> and the violent take it by force.

---

[41]Jesus is not the only one who casts out demons, for the children of his very detractors also perform exorcisms and, of necessity, through God's assistance. Are their exorcisms also a sign, like that of Jesus', of the breaking in of the kingdom of God? Siegfried Schulz, *Q. Die Spruchquelle der Evangelisten* (Zurich: Theologischer Verlag Zürich, 1972), p. 212, argues vigorously that while all exorcisms are from God, only Jesus' exorcisms bear an eschatological character, because he alone is the eschatological prophet, Son of God, and Son of Man, but Arland Dean Jacobson, *Wisdom Christology in Q* (diss. Claremont Graduate School, 1978; Ann Arbor, MI and London: University Microfilms International, 1981), p. 165, rightly points out that the eschatological uniqueness here lies not in the human person of Jesus or of the other exorcists, rather, in the Spirit of God that is operative in both; cf. Q 40.

Even though the precise meaning of this passage remains obscure, it does, nonetheless, clearly indicate that the kingdom of God is already present.

Another key passage for noting the presence of the kingdom of God is the twofold parable of the mustard seed and the leaven (Q 52):

> What is the kingdom of God like?
>   And to what shall I compare it?
> It is like a grain of mustard seed
>   which a man took and sowed in his field;
> and it grew and became a tree,
>   and the birds of the air made nests in its branches.
>
> To what shall I compare the kingdom of God?
> It is like leaven,
>   which a woman took and hid in three measures of meal,
>   till it was all leavened.

In this parable the kingdom is present in a small way, like a mustard seed and some leaven, but it becomes ever more widely manifest. What began with Jesus' ministry, in which he showed forth the beginning of the kingdom, is continued in the Q community, so that the once small manifestation of the kingdom becomes ever larger, like a mustard seed that becomes a tree or like the ever more pervasive effect of leaven in dough.

Significantly, we find another passage, this time in the mission section of Q, that serves as a bridge from the teaching of the presence of the kingdom to its future manifestation. Here we find Jesus instructing his disciples to continue his ministry of healing, a sign of the presence of the kingdom, and the preaching of the nearness of the kingdom of God in the future:

> And whenever you enter a town
>   and they receive you,
> heal the sick

and say to them,
  "The kingdom of God has come near to you."

Q 21 lines 12–16

The ministry of the disciples, including, of course, the members of the Q community, carries on the works of Jesus that indicate the presence of the kingdom and yet point to the fullness of the kingdom's manifestation in the future.

FUTURE MANIFESTATION OF THE KINGDOM

The closest that John the Baptist comes to preaching the kingdom in Q, besides the call to repentance, is his announcement of the coming of an apocalyptic figure who will carry out God's judgment. This apocalyptic figure will cut down trees and burn them, and he will be like a thresher who gathers his wheat but burns the chaff with unquenchable fire (Q 2). Such a dour portrayal of the future contrasts with Jesus' preaching of good news to the poor; John's preaching hardly encouraged listeners to hope in such an event, though the saving action of the coming One is not entirely suppressed, since the thresher will "gather his wheat." But Q does not say that John actually preached the kingdom, because it is clear from the rest of Q's presentation of the Baptist that John had an incomplete and inadequate understanding of what the kingdom is. (See the section entitled "John the Baptist's Relation to Jesus.")

Although Q also has Jesus speak of an apocalyptic figure who is coming to judge, namely, himself as son of man (We will discuss these passages further on.), the tenor of Jesus' ministry is more positive than John's. This was clear in the present manifestation of the kingdom in Jesus' words and deeds, but it is also true when he speaks of the future manifestation of the kingdom. For instance, the beatitudes of Q speak of the future blessings and comfort that will accompany the fullness of the kingdom of God:

> Blessed are the poor,
>   for theirs is the kingdom of God.
> Blessed are those who hunger now,
>   for they shall be satisfied.
> Blessed are those who weep now,
>   for they shall be comforted.
> Blessed are you when (people) hate you
>   and exclude and revile you
>   and utter evil against you
>   on account of the son of man.
> Rejoice and be glad,
>   for your reward is great in heaven:
>   for so their ancestors did to the prophets.
>
> Q 5 lines 4–16

It is likely that the first of these beatitudes, "Blessed are the poor, for theirs is the kingdom of God," is inclusive of the others,[42] so that the rest of the beatitudes (lines 6–16) speak of characteristics of the kingdom. It will be a time of happiness, which "blessed" means, and will be a state in which the hungry no longer lack food, the bereaved no longer sorrow, and heaven is offered as a reward to those who remain loyal to the teaching of the son of man (= Jesus), who speaks, in turn, for God. Heaven, then, is only part of the reign of God and is not synonymous with it (cf. also Q 44).

Another positive image of the future kingdom of God is that of the eschatological banquet. In Q 57 this comparison is told in the form of a story:

> A man gave a great banquet
>   and invited many,
>   and sent his servant to say to those who had been invited,

---

[42]See Francis Wright Beare, *The Gospel according to Matthew* (San Francisco: Harper & Row, Publishers, 1981), pp. 127–128: "In all [the beatitudes], the blessedness consists in participation in the kingdom of the heavens, and the entire sequence is bound together by this theme. It is not that the poor in spirit and the persecuted are assured of the Kingdom while the mourners, the pure in heart, the peacemakers and so forth receive a variety of different blessings. Those who are blessed are not various types; they are the same people, described in a variety of ways, and the rewards of life in the Kingdom are shared by all..."

"Come; for all is now ready,"
but they would not come.
. . .
> and the servant reported this to his master.

Then the householder in anger said to his servant,
> "Go out into the thoroughfares,
> and compel people to come in."

And the house was filled with guests.
I tell you,
> none of those invited shall taste my banquet.

Q 57

In the Q context it is clear that the man who gave the banquet represents God and his servant probably represents Wisdom or Jesus as Wisdom's agent.[43] The ministry of Jesus has been one of inviting people to share in the kingdom of God, "Come; for all is now ready." The response, of course, was one of rejection, whereupon the master (= God) told his servant to compel people to come in for their own sake. But this story ends with the harshness of judgment, another important aspect of the kingdom.

Although the kingdom of God has its positive side and Jesus even recommends to his disciples that they pray for the kingdom's arrival with the petition, "Thy kingdom come" (Q 26 line 4), nonetheless, the coming of the kingdom will also be a time of dread judgment. Therefore, in another passage about the eschatological banquet, we again find a threat at its conclusion:

> <I tell you
> that> many will come from east and west and sit at table
> > with Abraham, Isaac, and Jacob
> > and all the prophets in the kingdom of God,
> but you will be thrown into the outer darkness.
> There people will weep and gnash their teeth.

Q 55

[43]See the discussion in Paul Donald Meyer, "The Gentile Mission in Q," *Journal of Biblical Literature*, 89 (1970), 414–415.

This pericope is fascinating for several reasons. First, it indicates that the Q community understands itself to be among the prophets; second, the composition of the community may go beyond the Christian-Jews who are represented by the three great Jewish patriarchs, Abraham, Isaac and Jacob, for the community members come from everywhere (east and west), presumably including Gentiles; finally, the kingdom of God lasts beyond the judgment when some will be cast into the outer darkness where there will be weeping and gnashing of teeth—all images of the sorrow that will be experienced by those who do not participate in the reign of God.

It may seem surprising, at first, that Q does not use kingdom of God terminology with regard to judgment beyond what we have already noted. Even though Q has a great deal to say about the role of Jesus as an apocalyptic figure who plays a major part in judgment, it does not use the concept of kingdom of God in those sayings which speak of Jesus as this apocalyptic figure.[44] This curious separation of ideas in Q probably goes back to the ministry of Jesus, for he may not have spoken of himself as an apocalyptic figure to come at the end of time, but in view of his resurrection, which is never stated in Q but only presupposed, and the influence of John the Baptist's prophecy of the apocalyptic thresher, Jesus was identified by the Q community with the figure that John was awating. In doing this, the community respected the earlier Jesus traditions and did not associate kingdom terminology with this figure; yet, drawing upon Jesus' normal way of speaking about himself as "son of man," the community created sayings that spoke of Jesus as such an apocalyptic figure. The pre-resurrected Jesus, however, knew nothing of this identification. (For an analysis of the "son of man," designation, see the relevant material

---

[44]Philipp Vielhauer, "Gottesreich und Menschensohn in der Verkündigung Jesu," *Aufsätze zum Neuen Testament,* in: *Theologische Bücherei und Berichte aus dem 20. Jahrhundert,* 31, *Neues Testament* (Munich: Chr. Kaiser Verlag, 1965), pp. 55-91, made the important observation that the "kingdom of God" and "the coming Son of Man" concepts do not appear together in the preaching of Jesus.

under the section entitled, "The Person and the Role of Jesus in Q.")

IMMINENT JUDGMENT AND ITS DELAY

Having noted the twofold character of the kingdom of God in Q theology — its present manifestation in the ministry of Jesus and its future manifestation, we must now ask how these two aspects are related to one another. When will the judgment take place that climaxes in the complete manifestation of the kingdom?

For the most part, Q emphasizes an expectation of an imminent judgment, one which will take place soon and not in some far distant future.[45] We find this understanding already in Q's presentation of the preaching of John the Baptist. John's message bears a strong sense of urgency, because judgment is standing directly before him and his audience. He declares:

> Even now the axe is laid to the root of the trees;
>   every tree therefore that does not bear good fruit is
>   cut down
>   and thrown into the fire.

Q 2 lines 9–11

Not only is judgment imminent, it is also viewed as a threat of condemnation. Those who do not respond by repenting and bearing fruits of repentance will be thrown into the fire like a tree that produces no good fruit.

This threat of imminent judgment is accompanied by a

---

[45]Throughout this discussion on the imminent judgment and the nature of its delay, I have borrowed extensively from Paul Hoffmann, *Studien zur Theologie der Logienquelle*, in: *Neutestamentliche Abhandlungen*, Neue Folge, 8 (Münster: Verlag Aschendorf, 1972), pp. 26-50. His argumentation contrasts especially with that of Dieter Lührmann, *Die Redaktion der Logienquelle*, in: *Wissenschaftliche Monographien zum Alten und Neuen Testament*, 33 (Neukirchen-Vluyn: Neukirchner Verlag, 1969), pp. 69-89, who emphasizes the importance of the delay of the parousia, which also affects his later dating of Q.

particular interest in the person of the coming judge. In the
present form of the Q text, this figure is portrayed as mightier and worthier than John, one who will baptize with the
holy Spirit and fire. He is also portrayed as an apocalyptic
thresher who is ready to work in the gathering of the wheat,
already holding the winnowing fork in his hand. Here too
we sense the urgency and find the threat of condemnation,
for this apocalyptic thresher will burn the useless chaff with
unquenchable fire.

In taking over these traditions of the Baptist's preaching
and, perhaps, here and there adding to them, the Q community has shown that this preaching maintains its validity
for its own audience. There is no attempt on the part of Q to
mitigate its intensity, and we find the threefold concerns of
John's preaching, namely, imminence, threat of judgment
and an apocalyptic judge, elsewhere in Q but not always
together nor with equal clarity, especially with regard to the
imminence of the coming judgment.

In the section of Q which Polag entitles "The Mission of
the Disciples" (Q 17-25), the disciples are being admonished
by Jesus to offer the greeting of peace, to heal the sick, and
to announce the nearness of the reign of God: "The kingdom
of God has come near to you" (Q 21 line 16; cf. also lines
3–15). Since the kingdom in its final manifestation is near
and because judgment initiates this phase of the kingdom,
this passage underscores the imminent judgment as well.

Corresponding to this is the time of the final harvest of
God that is being gathered now. It stands in need of more
harvesters because the crop is plentiful and the time is short:

> The harvest is plentiful, but the laborers are few;
> pray therefore the Lord of the harvest
>   to send out laborers into his harvest.

Q 18 lines 4–6

Again in Q 21 which speaks of the nearness of the kingdom, we find the threat of judgment associated with it for
those who reject the message:

> But whenever you enter a town
>> and they do not receive you,
> as you leave that town
>> shake off the dust from your feet.
> I tell you
>> that it shall be more tolerable on that day for Sodom
>> than for that town.

Q 21 lines 17–22

Even as this unnamed town may conceivably have rejected the messengers of Jesus' teaching and is, therefore, threatened with imminent judgment, so we must probably understand the same set of circumstances to be in effect for the saying of Q 22. This passage names certain specific towns that have rejected the message and have not repented:

> Woe to you, Chorazin!
>> Woe to you, Bethsaida!
> For if in Tyre and Sidon
>> had been done the works done in you,
>> they would have repented long ago in sackcloth and ashes.
> But I tell you,
>> it shall be more tolerable in the judgment for Tyre and Sidon
>> than for you.
> And you, Capernaum, will you be exalted to heaven?
>> You shall be brought down to Hades.

Q 22

The context of Q requires the interpretation of an imminent judgment for this saying, even though the saying by itself says nothing about the time element; there is, however, a certain intensity akin to urgency in its formulation.

The apocalyptic figure associated with judgment and first prophesied by John appears in some passages of Q where Jesus speaks of himself as "son of man" (Q 39, 46, 69, 70), but none of these passages clearly speaks of that figure's coming as imminent. Only Q 42 (which Polag holds to belong to Q, although it is found only in the special Matthaean material) indicates the imminent coming of Jesus. This coming will occur before the disciples (= Q prophets) have preached their message in all the towns of Israel:

> [When they persecute you in one town,
>   flee to the next;
> truly, I say to you,
> you will not have gone through all the towns of Israel
>   before the son of man comes.]

Q 42

Seemingly contradicting the imminent judgment, one of the "son of man" sayings listed above (Q 46) points to some sort of time lapse before the arrival of this apocalyptic figure. In this parabolic saying it is implied that the householder has indeed left his house, confident that the thief would not come. The point is that the parousia has not occurred, and some people are no longer expecting it to happen:

> But know this,
> that if the householder had known
>   at what hour the thief was coming,
>   he would not have left his house to be broken into.
> Therefore, you also must be ready,
>   for the son of man is coming at an hour you do not expect.

Q 46

The conclusion of the saying does not argue against a delay but against the notion that the parousia may never happen. Because it will happen, however, one should be ready for it even when uncertain as to when precisely it will occur.

Another parabolic saying, which in the order of Q sayings follows the previously discussed passage, speaks even more clearly of a delay:

Who then is the faithful and wise servant,
   whom the master has set over his household,
      to give them their food at the proper time?
Blessed is that servant
   whom the master, when he comes, will find doing so.
Truly, I say to you,
he will set that servant over all his possessions.

But if that servant thinks,
   "My master is delayed in coming,"
      and begins to beat the other servants,
         and eats and drinks with the drunken,
the master of that servant will come
   on a day when he is not expected and at an hour that
      is not known,
         and will punish that one
            and place that one among the unfaithful.

Q 47

Like Q 46, the time of the parousia is not known, but the coming will surely happen, even when people mistakenly assume that is has been delayed. The same thoughts, no doubt, lie behind yet a third parabolic saying, namely, the lengthy story of Q 75.

Two more passages may be cited as evidence for the delay of the parousia (Q 45, 70), but it is uncertain whether Q 45 belongs to Q, since the passage is special Lucan material. In the case of Q 70, the crucial lines (6–7) are again special Lucan material.

Since we noted earlier that Q stressed the imminence of judgment, how are we to understand the presence of materials that point to a delay of that event? An answer to this question depends on how the delay is interpreted. The biblical Gospels of Matthew and Luke have taken up these sayings that speak of delay and interpreted them to mean a relatively lengthy period of time. For Matthew the parousia will not occur until after the gospel has been proclaimed to the whole world (Matt. 28:19-20). For Luke the time of delay is likewise indistinct, but according to him the gospel must first proceed from Jerusalem to Rome and throughout the Roman Empire, which is the very schema of the Book of Acts (1:8). In both cases the delay is, indeed, a long delay. But in the case of Q, there is no need to read into the document what Matthew and Luke have done with those sayings, for it is quite possible to understand them in the framework of the imminent judgment. In this view, the delay must be understood to occur only within the span of a lifetime or the length of a particular generation. Q theology does not necessarily contradict itself on this important issue, and the Q community as reflected in the text of Q as we now have it probably remained thoroughly imbued with the imminent judgment.

John the Baptist's Relation to Jesus in Q

John the Baptist has always been at best an enigmatic figure for Christianity and at worst an embarrassment. If the Baptist had really recognized who Jesus was as Messiah, as he so clearly does in the Gospel of John, then it is indeed difficult to understand why the disciples of John did not all become disciples of Jesus. In fact, we know that even after the deaths of John and Jesus, the Baptist's disciples continued to exist as a group in rivalry with Christianity.[46] This leads us to suspect that the historical John the Baptist may have been "Christianized" by early Christian writers such as the four evangelists. The same is true for the author of Q, but the Q document retains more of the rougher edges of the "pre-Christianized" Baptist.

Although John appears or is mentioned only a few times in Q, nonetheless, he is second only to Jesus in importance, and about a tenth of Q is devoted to materials concerning him. In Polag's reconstruction of Q, there are two major blocks of Baptist material, a group of sayings at the very

---

[46]See H.H. Scobie, *John the Baptist* (Philadelphia: Fortress Press, 1964), pp. 187–202.

beginning of Q, namely Q 1, 2 and 3, and a second group, namely Q 14, 15 and 16, that occurs in the midst of Jesus' preaching while John is being held in prison. Finally, John is also named in Q 62.

In the first set of Baptist sayings, we learn that John was preaching (a baptism of) repentance in the wilderness of the Jordan region. As such, he is presented as fulfilling an Old Testament prophecy, "A voice of one crying in the wilderness, 'Prepare the way of the Lord, make his paths straight.'" Originally this Old Testament quotation referred to the coming of God (= Yahweh) — not Jesus. It is not clear that "Lord" refers to Jesus here either, although that is often the interpretation given it. The better understanding of the prophecy in this context, however, seems to be as a reference to the Lord God, for John is basically preparing the way for God's judgment.

John's preaching points to the end time which he describes as "the wrath to come," and he understands that end time to be imminent. Therefore, he says, "even now the axe is laid to the root of the trees." This end time will be accompanied by the arrival of an apocalyptic figure whom John describes as one mightier than himself and whose sandal thong he is not worthy to untie. This apocalyptic figure will undertake two activities in that end time. First, he will baptize with the holy Spirit[47] and with fire, and second, he will do threshing, that is, gathering his wheat into the granary and burning the chaff with unquenchable fire. The implication of this saying is that those who repent and bear the fruits of repentance will be saved; those who do not repent will perish, and it is not enough to expect salvation merely through physical association with the historical Israel which claims Abraham as its father.

The tone of John's speech is intense and strident, an example of fire and brimstone preaching. He comes off as a doomsday preacher, addressing his audience hostilely as a "brood of vipers," and by haranguing and frightening them,

[47] An earlier version of the saying, "He will baptize you with the holy Spirit and with fire," (Q 2 line 16), may have spoken of a "baptism with wind (= spirit) and fire," referring entirely to the final judgment; see Jacobson, p. 33.

he hopes to bring them to repentance. In Q John's baptism is not only not emphasized (He is not even called "the Baptist") but purposely deemphasized. John may be inveighing against a notion that his baptism is an automatic satisfaction for wrong-doing and is sufficient for repentance; rather, John is more interested in his hearers bearing the fruits of repentance.[48]

In Q 3 the scene shifts to that of Jesus' baptism. Jesus comes to be baptized by John.[49] The purpose for Jesus receiving baptism is not stated, though it would seem that he, like the others who came to John, came for the baptism of repentance. In this regard, it should not be forgotten that Q knows of no infancy narrative about Jesus; it knows nothing of his virginal conception nor of his sinlessness. Indeed, only following the baptism of repentance is Jesus declared by the voice from heaven (= God) to be his Son. In what sense Q understands Jesus to be God's Son will be treated later.

Significantly the words of the heavenly voice are addressed only to Jesus and, presumably, only he has heard the voice. John, on the other hand, does not know this, for he has heard nothing and has not shared in the vision. John does not yet know that Jesus' baptism experience was different from anyone else's.

Given the Q portrayal of John the Baptist up to this point, where John has made no special connection with his preaching and his baptism of repentance to the person of Jesus, it is understandable why John later sends two of his disciples to Jesus to ask him, "Are you the one who is to come or shall

[48]Jacobson, pp. 30–31.

[49]Although Polag includes the "baptism of Jesus" pericope among the Q sayings, most scholars disagree. Detailed reasons for its inclusion are provided by Polag, *Die Christologie*, pp. 151–154, and by Jacobson, pp. 35–36. The baptism account appears in the reconstruction of Q by J.M.C. Crum, *The Original Jerusalem Gospel. Being Essays on the Document Q* (London: Constable & Company LTD, 1927), p. 129 and by Archibald M. Hunter, *The Work and Words of Jesus*, rev. ed. (Philadelphia: The Westminster Press, 1973), p. 166. Adolf Harnack, *New Testament Studies, II. The Sayings of Jesus. The Second Source of St. Matthew and St. Luke*, in: *Crown Theological Library*, 23. trans. J.R. Wilkinson (New York: G.P. Putnam's Sons, 1908), p. 254, includes the baptism of Jesus in brackets, indicating his uncertainty as to whether it belonged to Q.

we look for another?" (Q 14). During his imprisonment
John has heard about the things Jesus has been saying and
doing. It is in Jesus' response and the sayings that follow (Q
14–16) that we most clearly see the enigma or embarrassment of John's presence in the tradition.

In the Q presentation, John did not know who Jesus was
nor did he see any connection between Jesus and the apocalyptic figure he was expecting. The things that John may
have heard about Jesus (Q only relates Jesus' sermon on the
mount and his healing of the centurion's servant, nos. 5-13)
have some parallels to his own preaching in terms of ethical
exhortation, but except for the phrase, "You hypocrite" (Q
10 line 5), the tone of Jesus' preaching is very different from
John's. It is not hostile; it is not even very apocalyptic.
Instead, Jesus summarizes his ministry in the message that is
to be sent back to John:

> Go and tell John what you see and hear:
> the blind receive their sight and the lame walk,
> lepers are cleansed and the deaf hear,
> the dead are raised up, and the poor have good news
>   preached to them,
> and whoever takes no offense at me is blessed.
>
> Q 14

What John hears from Jesus is a description of a ministry
consisting of healing and the proclamation of good news to
the poor. No doubt, this answer was perplexing to John (in
the way Q portrays him), because this contrasts sharply with
the kind of figure that John was expecting. While the Spirit
may have been operative in Jesus' ministry, John certainly
would have wondered where the baptism of fire and the
thresher of the end time were.

That John may never have understood the meaning of
Jesus and his ministry is indicated in the next passage (Q 15)
where Jesus at first praises John as a prophet, saying that
"among those born of women there has risen no one greater
than John." Then, despite this admiration for the man, who
may have been his own teacher, Jesus also says of John that

"whoever is least in the kingdom of God is greater than he."
The impact of these latter words is that John stands outside
of God's kingdom. John does not yet understand the meaning of Jesus and his ministry; he has not understood that
with the person and ministry of Jesus, the kingdom of God
has already begun to break in. John has not recognized
Jesus as the agent of God's kingdom nor the signs that he
performed nor his message as manifestations of the kingdom.
Indeed, Q never has John proclaim the kingdom of God.
Therefore, despite all his greatness, John is still an unbe-
liever, and for this reason, anyone who does accept Jesus
and the kingdom of God proclaimed by him is greater than
John.

This negative evaluation of John is balanced off, in part,
by Jesus' previous affirmation of John's positive role as the
greatest of the prophets, as God's messenger preparing the
way. His preaching begins a new era, for "the law and the
prophets were until John" (Q 62). He enabled Jesus to
manifest God's kingdom, even when John himself did not
adequately understand what was happening. Therefore,
John has played an important but marred role in salvation
history.

Q contains one other positive statement about John (Q
16) in which Jesus contrasts himself with John. They are
antithetically parallel in the negative response each elicits as
a prophet. The people of "this generation" have, on one
hand, charged John with having a demon because of his
ascetical life, neither eating nor drinking and, on the other,
they have claimed Jesus to be something of a party boy who
mixes with the dregs of society, eating and drinking too
much. So the children of Wisdom, John and Jesus, have
been rejected by "this generation", though this rejection
does not affect the validity of their wisdom.

After these observations Q has no more interest in John,
and we do not even learn what happened to John after his
imprisonment, as we do in the Synoptics.[50] Nor do we find
John explicitly pointing to Jesus as "the lamb of God"

---

[50]Mark 6:14–29; Matthew 14:1–12; Luke 9:7–9; 3:19–20.

before whom he must decrease while Jesus must increase, as in the Gospel of John.[51] Instead, Q simply drops John from consciousness.

An important question arises from this: if John the Baptist was not perceived by the author(s) of Q as a believer in the message of Jesus, why has he been given such a prominent place in Q itself? It is likely that John's importance to the historical person of Jesus and the influence of the disciples of John at the time of the final redaction of Q were principal factors. One other point may have also played a significant role in the preservation of the Baptist material in Q, and that is the increased apocalyptic interest in the Q community. The community's creation of the so-called futuristic son of man sayings, in which Jesus is portrayed as coming in the end time fits together with John the Baptist's notion of the apocalyptic figure that would usher in the last time. Thus it may have been the increased post-resurrectional interest in an apocalyptic end time that helped preserve the memory of John. The result, then, is that while John misunderstood Jesus and his mission, so Jesus did not fully comprehend his own role as apocalyptic savior. The redactor of Q, however, standing at some distance away from both John and Jesus could see the fullness of John's role in salvation history in a way the historical Jesus could not.

The Person and Role of Jesus in Q

In all four of our biblical Gospels, Jesus, the proclaimer, becomes the one who is proclaimed, but in Q he remains the proclaimer. In fact, the primary theological thrust of the Q document is the continuation of the message that Jesus proclaimed, and this contrasts significantly with our biblical Gospels which emphasize the person and deeds of Jesus as the content of the proclamation itself. Yet, even though Jesus is certainly proclaiming everywhere in Q, a closer

[51]John 1:29–31; 3:27–30.

examination of the Q sayings reveals that the person and role of Jesus cannot easily be separated from his message. These sayings reveal that the proclaimer is indeed intimately associated with his proclamation. Therefore it is important that we do not overlook the significance of the person and role of Jesus in Q.[52]

JESUS AS THE PROPHETIC SON OF GOD

When Jesus first appears in Q, it is at his baptism at the hands of John (Q 3). Jesus is presumably not only washed clean of sin, as John's baptism for repentance assumes, but more importantly, we have the introduction of the Spirit and the heavenly voice (= God) that declares Jesus to be *his* Son. We must not conclude too readily from this that Jesus in understood to be the Messiah, for Q never calls Jesus "the Christ;" the name "Christ" (= Messiah or "anointed one") does not appear at all in Q. Instead, the pericope of the baptism of Jesus says nothing about the nature of this sonship or what it means that Jesus possesses the Spirit. For this information we must look elsewhere in Q.

In the very next passage, the temptation of Jesus (Q 4), we learn more about the Spirit and Jesus' sonship. The Spirit leads him into the desert, the place of spiritual combat, the place where John before him had lived as a prophet. The implication of this is that Jesus is a prophet too, and even more than a prophet because he is also God's Son.[53] What was said about the sonship of Jesus in the baptism pericope is repeated here in the temptation story, where the devil in dialogue with Jesus twice says, "If you are Son of God..." Jesus does not answer that he is, although in the sequence of Q he already knows that he is God's Son. In the temptation story Jesus demonstrates that fact but without stating it. Inspired by God, Jesus quotes scripture authoritatively to

[52]Ivan Havener, "Jesus in the Gospel Sayings," *The Bible Today*, 21 (March 1983), 77–82.

[53]Jacobson, p. 37, recognizes the John/desert—Jesus/desert parallel, but Polag, *Die Christologie*, p. 147, sees, a contrast here between God's loyal Son Jesus in the desert and God's disloyal son Israel in the desert.

oppose the devil, and he does not give in to the devil's temptations. Possessed by the Spirit, he understands God and even identifies himself with the Lord God in the sense of speaking God's word, being God's agent. What Jesus says, therefore, is to be listened to not merely because of the quality and content of the message itself but precisely because Jesus has a special relationship to God which makes his teaching authoritative. In other words, the person of Jesus cannot be separated here from the message he proclaims. Jesus is God's inspired, prophetic Son.

While Jesus is recognized by the supernatural powers (the voice from heaven and the devil) as God's Son, Jesus identifies himself as God's prophetic Son not only in combat with the devil but in his preaching to people. In Q's sermon on the mount (Q 5-12), Jesus preaches authoritatively as God's agent to humans. He announces who will have a share in God's kingdom:

> Blessed are the poor,
>   for theirs is the kingdom of God.
> Blessed are those who hunger now,
>   for they shall be satisfied.
> Blessed are those who weep now,
>   for they shall be comforted.
> Blessed are you when (people) hate you
>   and exclude and revile you
>   and utter evil against you
>   on account of the son of man.
> Rejoice and be glad,
> for your reward is great in heaven:
>   for so their ancestors did to the prophets.

Q 5

Because suffering on account of the son of man (= Jesus) is a source of blessedness, it is clear that acknowledgement of Jesus leads to participation in the kingdom of God. In underscoring that attacks have been made on prophets before him, the passage identifies Jesus as a prophet as well, with the implication that his followers are prophets too.

Not only do those who listen to Jesus become prophets like him, but they also become "sons of God,"[54] even as he is God's Son:

> [I say to you,]
> love your enemies
> and you will be sons of God . . .

Q 6 lines 20–22

Listening to Jesus in the sense of obeying him is not a matter of indifference, for those who do what Jesus says are like a man who builds his house on a solid rock, for such a one is preserved from the elements of destruction (Q 12). Those who believe in Jesus' authority receive the benefits of the manifestation of God's kingdom. Clearly, the message of Jesus cannot be separated from his person.

This special role of Jesus in initiating God's kingdom is also seen in his response to John the Baptist's question from prison (Q 14). Jesus not only tells John the things he preaches but also what he does. While these deeds are not said to have been performed by Jesus alone, the conclusion to this passage focuses on the person of Jesus: "And whoever takes no offense at me is blessed." Jesus is indeed the one who is coming now, in the present, but one who is quite different from the apocalyptic figure that John the Baptist was expecting.

The special relationship of Jesus to God is underscored again in the Beelzebul controversy story (Q 29). In this pericope Jesus shows his critics the flaw in their logic: it would make no sense for him to cast out demons by the prince of demons, since the devil would then be defeating his own purpose. Jesus' exorcisms have a very different source; therefore, he declares: "But if it is by the finger of God that I

---

[54]I have purposely not translated "sons" as "children," because it is crucial to see the technical connection between Jesus the "Son of God" and the members of the Q community who are also "sons of God," in that they, like Jesus, and through him have become God's adopted children.

cast out demons, then the kingdom of God has come upon you." Jesus' deeds are indicative that God is manifesting his kingdom now through the person of Jesus, for he is God's agent.

The uniqueness of Jesus' relation to God is disclosed in Q 24, which speaks of the Son and the Father. While we have already noted the baptism and temptation stories where Jesus is referred to as God's Son, only this passage uses the "Son" designation in an unique sense and it appears on the lips of Jesus himself:

> All things have been delivered to me by my Father;
> and no one knows the Son except the Father,
> no one the Father except the Son
> and anyone to whom the Son chooses to reveal him.

Q 24

This passage proclaims that Jesus is God's Son and that only by accepting the Son as the revealer of God the Father can God be known. Thus only with this knowledge can one enter the kingdom of God. This is the very heart of Q's understanding of the way of salvation. Jesus himself is the very means of salvation, but it is not through his redeeming death, which is nowhere mentioned in Q, rather, in his revealing of God's reign and of the way to share in that kingdom. In other words, the Son reveals the Father to others, and those, to whom the Son chooses to reveal the Father, also know the Father like the Son. In this sense they become real "sons of God" themselves, cf. Q 6 line 22. On the other hand, those who reject Jesus are, in effect, also rejecting the Father who sent him: ". . . whoever rejects me rejects him who sent me" (Q 23 line 3). Of course, the sending from the Father does not refer to the incarnation of Jesus but to Jesus' call to be a prophet. Those who do not reject but see and hear what Jesus does and says are blessed more than the prophets and kings of old (Q 25) because these seers and hearers share in Jesus' sonship.

JESUS AS THE SON OF MAN

This prophetic sonship of Jesus which has just been discussed has often been overshadowed in discussions of Q theology by a focus on Jesus as "son of man." One of the reasons for this special attention is that "son of man" is the most frequent designation of Jesus in Q, even as it is often used for him in the biblical Gospels.

Before examining the Q passages that speak of the son of man, we should be aware of some other curious facts about this designation. It appears virtually exclusively on the lips of Jesus in the Gospels, but the term never appears in the writings of Paul and those ascribed to him. It is found in only four New Testament passages outside the Gospels, namely, Acts 7:56; Heb. 2:6; Apoc. 1:13; 14:14. Beyond the New Testament it appears only once in the letters of Ignatius of Antioch (IgnEph. 20:2), once in the Epistle of Barnabas (12:10), and once in Eusebius' *Church History* (II 23, 13), where he is quoting, in turn, from Hegesippus' report on the martyrdom of James. Only in the Gnostic and sectarian writings cited by Irenaeus and Hippolytus, and, of course, in the Nag Hammadi literature do we find frequent use of the term.[55] This raises the intriguing question: if the son of man designation was the most important one for Jesus in Q and in the Synoptic tradition, why was its use so insignificant in the church at large? Whether this question remains a paradox of fact or admits an answer depends on how the son of man designation is understood.

In Q there are two kinds of son of man sayings, one group which speaks of the present, earthly activities of the son of man (Q 5 lines 10ff.; Q 16, 17, 33, 40) and one which speaks of the the future, apocalyptic actions of the son of man (Q 39, 46, 69 lines 6 ff, Q 70; cf. also Q 42 which Polag includes in his reconstruction but which is found only in Matthew's Gospel). Unlike Mark and the other Synoptics, there are no

---

[55]See the discussion of the Nag Hammadi passages that speak of the son of man in Frederick Houk Borsch, *The Christian and Gnostic Son of Man*, in: *Studies in Biblical Theology*, Second Series, 14 (Naperville, IL: Alec R. Allenson, Inc., 1970), espec. 58–121.

son of man sayings in Q that speak of the suffering and/or resurrection of the son of man, such as we find, for instance in Mark 9:31:

> For he was teaching his disciples, saying to them,
> "The son of man will be delivered into the hands of men,
>   and they will kill him;
> and when he is killed,
>   after three days he will rise."

The dominant scholarly view of the last twenty-five years is that the son of man sayings have their earliest form in the future, apocalyptic sayings that speak of the parousia, that is, of the arrival of the son of man at the end time. There are, however, two primary variants of this theory.

The earlier point of view held that indeed the historical Jesus used "son of man" as a title but not for himself.[56] In other words, he made a distinction between himself and this son of man who was to come. Thus in Q 39, "But I tell you, every one who acknowledges me before others, the son of man also will acknowledge before the angels of God," Jesus speaks of himself only in the first half of the saying, but he is speaking of someone other than himself as the son of man in the second half of the saying. According to the proponents of this point of view, it was only after the resurrection of Jesus that the early church identified Jesus with this coming son of man. It then read this title back into the pre-resurrection life of Jesus, so that Jesus would on occasion speak of his earthly activities as son of man. Still later, beyond Q, the title became associated with sayings which spoke of Jesus' suffering and/or resurrection.

A variant of this view holds that the son of man sayings developed in the same chronological order, namely, first the future, apocalyptic parousia sayings, second, the earthly activities sayings, and finally, the suffering and/or resurrec-

---

[56]Heinz Eduard Tödt, *The Son of Man in the Synoptic Tradition*, in: *The New Testament Library*, trans. Dorothea M. Barton (Philadelphia: The Westminster Press, 1965), espec. pp. 55–60, 64–67, 250–274. This book, more than any other, gave impetus to serious scholarly work on the theology of Q.

tion sayings. The difference in this point of view is that it denies that the historical Jesus ever used even the parousia sayings at all.[57] The reason for denying this is the correct observation that Jesus nowhere speaks of the coming of the kingdom of God, which is the primary content of his preaching, with the coming of a son of man. The two concepts, kingdom of God and the coming son of man, are not combined together either in Q or Mark. The upshot of all this is that the proponents of this view hold that none of the son of man sayings go back to the historical Jesus; all of them are products of the early church.

This dominant view in both of its forms holds that the son of man designation is a Christological title, which is based on an apocalyptic son of man figure as we find it in Daniel 7:13 and in the extra-biblical writings of 4 Esdras and the Similitudes of Ethiopic I Enoch.[58] Apocalyptic is seen as the context or *Sitz im Leben* for the son of man concept as it is used in the New Testament. Only after Jesus was identified with this coming son of man figure following his resurrection was the title son of man read back into sayings about his earthly life. For the proponents of this view, the son of man title remains the key to understanding the person of Jesus in Q theology.

In more recent times, another possibility has been given renewed credibility. According to this alternative, it is the earthly activities son of man sayings that provide a link to the historical Jesus,[59] but "son of man" itself is not a title at all.[60] In Aramaic, the language that Jesus probably spoke,

[57]Vielhauer, "Gottesreich und Menschensohn in der Verkündigung Jesu," pp. 55–91, and in the same book of essays, "Jesus und der Menschensohn. Zur Diskussion mit Heinz Eduard Tödt und Eduard Schweizer," pp. 92-140.

[58]See Tödt, pp. 21–31; Ferdinand Hahn, *The Titles of Jesus in Christology. Their History in Early Christianity*, trans. Harold Knight and George Ogg (New York: World Publishing Co., 1969), pp. 15–21, and Reginald H. Fuller, *The Foundations of New Testament Christology* (New York: Charles Scribner's Sons, 1965), pp. 34–43.

[59]T.W. Manson, *The Teaching of Jesus. Studies of Its Form and Content*, 2nd ed. (Cambridge: Cambridge University Press, 1963 [= 1935]), pp. 211-234, acknowledges that Jesus used "son of man" in speaking of himself during his earthly ministry.

[60]The non-titular understanding of "son of man" has most forcefully been

"son of man" can simply mean "someone" including the speaker, or it can also mean the speaker himself, that is, another way of saying "I".

Proponents of this view have correctly noted that son of man is not a title for an individual figure in the Jewish apocalyptic writing of Daniel. Instead, Daniel 7:13 speaks of "one like a son of man," and this is a reference to the "saints of the Most High," a composite being. Besides this, only Daniel among the apocalyptic Jewish son of man sources certainly predates Q (and Mark), whereas 4 Esdras and I Enoch[61] are writings either contemporary with or even later than Q. This means that there is no extant concept of an individual apocalyptic son of man figure that predates Q.

Since Q never quotes Daniel 7:13 nor even clearly alludes to the passage, it is difficult to speak of a Christian midrash, that is, an explanatory interpretation in rabbinic fashion, of Daniel 7:13 in the Q parousia son of man sayings. Indeed, the Christological significance of son of man is greatly diminished, if it is not associated with a figure that everyone was expecting or knew about by that name, and it cannot be overlooked that Jesus is never challenged by his opponents because he is the son of man; rather, it is always for other

argued by Geza Vermes who proceeds from the Aramaic background of this terminology. The importance of his findings for Q theology, a topic he himself does not directly address, is nothing less than revolutionary; see his essays: "The Use of *Bar Nash/Bar Nasha* in Jewish Aramaic," Appendix E in Matthew Black's *An Aramaic Approach to the Gospels and Acts*, 3rd ed. (Oxford: Clarendon Press, 1967), pp. 310–330; "Jesus the *Son of Man*" in his book, *Jesus the Jew. A Historian's Reading of the Gospels* (London: Fontana/Collins, 1973), pp. 160–191, and "The 'Son of Man' Debate," *Journal for the Study of the New Testament*, 1 (1978), 19–32.

[61] The portions of I Enoch uncovered at Qumran do not include the Similitudes in which the son of man sayings appear. George W.E. Nickelsburg, *Jewish Literature between the Bible and the Mishnah* (Philadelphia: Fortress Press, 1981), p. 150, says that we can be almost certain that these similitudes (or parables) did not belong to the same Qumran manuscripts as the portions that are now extant; see the detailed discussion on the dating of the Similitudes of Enoch in George R. Beasley-Murray's, "Excursus 1. The Date of the Similitudes of Enoch," *Jesus and the Kingdom of God* (Grand Rapids: William B. Eerdmans Publishing Company, 1986), pp. 63–68. Jacobson, p. 16, is correct when he notes that "it is increasingly doubtful whether it is proper to speak of a 'concept' of the Son of Man, as though it were a fixed idea inherited from Jewish apocalyptic. There is no real consistency in the use of the title in Jewish apocalyptic...". One must ask now whether the term is a title at all, especially in Q.

reasons that he comes into conflict with them. This is exactly what we might expect if the son of man terminology was used in ordinary speech without any apocalyptic or other titular associations.

Our purpose here is not to try to determine what sayings may go back to the historical Jesus, but one observation seems in order. Because of Jesus' own eschatological, but only mildly apocalyptic, teaching[62] and the observation that the coming of the kingdom of God is not associated with the coming of the son of man in that teaching, none of the future, apocalyptic son of man sayings can be said to go back to the historical Jesus. On the other hand, the earthly activities son of man sayings could possibly go back to the historical person of Jesus. This would help to explain why there are so many son of man sayings, for this terminology was the way Jesus often referred to himself. The early church, in this case the Q community, reflecting on the meaning of Jesus at a later time, created sayings in the manner of Jesus' usual way of speaking. In this way, son of man sayings were multiplied. Because this designation was not a title for Jesus, there is no reason to suspect that it was ever understood as a title in Q either. This would help to explain why Paul and most other early Christian writers did not use the son of man designation: it was not a title in their understanding either; rather it was merely a common way that Jesus spoke of himself.

An important question remains to be answered concerning Q's use of son of man: why did the Q community associate Jesus with the apocalyptic figure who would play such a significant role in the judgment at the end time? We alluded to an answer at the conclusion of our discussion of the kingdom of God but review its points here in more detail.

[62]Eschatology is the teaching concerning the final age,whereas apocalyptic is a form of eschatology that frequently deals with a cataclysmic end of the world. The teaching of Jesus was clearly eschatological, but the apocalyptic elements were not emphasized as strongly, as we find them, for instance, in the Book of the Apocalypse.

There seem to be at least three possible circumstances that gave rise to the identification of Jesus with this apocalyptic figure. The first of these is the presupposition of Jesus' resurrection. Jesus can return as an apocalyptic figure, because he is still alive. His prophetic sonship is unique, for although he is a prophet, he is more than a prophet; he is also God's Son, but he possesses a sonship that is special and like no one else's relation to God. The resurrection only serves to underscore that unique relationship to God, taking over some of God's own judging capacities. Seen in this light, the identification of Jesus with this figure seems to make good sense.

The second contributing factor may very well be the preaching of John the Baptist about the coming of an apocalyptic judge. Despite the fact that historically Jesus and John may have disagreed on this issue, it was ironically Jesus' own praise of John that lent credence to John's preaching in the eyes of the Q community. In the light of Jesus' resurrection and the preaching of John, whose person Jesus highly praised, the Q community understood Jesus to be the apocalyptic figure about whom John had foretold.

But a third factor may also have given rise to this identification, namely, a crisis within the Q community itself that fostered an apocalyptic manner of thinking. Apocalyptic ideas often intensify under trying circumstances, and there is plenty of evidence in Q that the Q prophets were experiencing the rejection of their message, even as Jesus' message had been rejected before theirs and as John the Baptist's message had been rejected before that of Jesus. The anxiety and frustration of the community may, therefore, have led to an emphasis on the nearing end time and upon the hope for the fullness of the kingdom of God's manifestation, a time when the enemies of the community's message would be decisively condemned and the proclaimers of the kingdom of God who acknowledge Jesus as God's agent would be vindicated with the other prophets at the eschatological banquet.

JESUS AS THE AGENT OF WISDOM

Not only did Q preserve a number of wise sayings in the form of proverbs and maxims that Jesus is said to have spoken, but some of the materials of Q also reveal a special relationship of Jesus to personified Wisdom herself. In order to understand how such a relationship was conceived, we need first to know something about the Jewish tradition of speculative Wisdom.

The roots of the speculative Wisdom tradition go back to Jewish sources, some of which are biblical like the Book of Proverbs and Job or are deutero-canonical, writings such as Sirach, Wisdom of Solomon, Baruch,[63] or are considered "extra-biblical" such as I Enoch and 4 Esdras. While these and similar texts are relatively late Jewish writings in comparison with other Old Testament works, nonetheless, most of them predated Q, with I Enoch and 4 Esdras possibly being exceptions.

From these writings we can arrive at a composite picture of Wisdom motifs, though no single text brings all of them together. Charles E. Carlston[64] has summarized these motifs in the following manner:

> Wisdom was created by God in the beginning; hidden with God and dwelling in the heavens; wisdom was present at the Creation, in which she served as agent (or instrument); she came to earth, sent to call both Israel and all humankind, some of whom listened to her, but most of whom did not; rejected by humanity and finding no place of rest, she returned to dwell with God.

Not all of these motifs are found in Q, such as Wisdom as the agent of creation, but several others are apparent in passages that also have a bearing on the person and role of Jesus.

[63]These deutero-canonical writings are found in Roman Catholic and Eastern Orthodox bibles but are called "apocryphal" writings by Protestants and "extra-canonical" writings by Jews. Neither Protestants nor Jews consider these writings a part of the biblical canon.

[64]Carlston, pp. 101–102.

While not exhausting all the passages in Q that bear on these Wisdom motifs, four of them stand out in particular, and we will look briefly at each of them: Q 16, 24, 36, 51.[65]

We have already met the first of these passages, Q 16, in our discussion of the relation of John the Baptist to Jesus. In this case, we want to especially note the Wisdom motifs that are to be found in it:

> To what then shall I compare this generation
>   and what is it like?
> It is like children sitting in the market place
>   and calling to their playmates — they say,
>   "We piped to you, and you did not dance;
>   We wailed, and you did not mourn."
> For John came neither eating nor drinking,
>   and you say, "He has a demon."
> The son of man came eating and drinking,
>   and you say, "Behold, a glutton and a drunkard,
>   a friend of tax collectors and sinners."
> Yet wisdom is justified by her children.

Q 16

The final line speaks of personified Wisdom, and her children are John the Baptist and Jesus. It is through them that she (= Wisdom) is justified, because they have received her at her coming, while "this generation" has rejected her and is now portrayed as a group of recalcitrant playmates who do not respond to the calls of others. The same dynamics are repeated in the case of the coming of John and Jesus, for again "this generation" rejects them both, mocking each in the process. Because John and Jesus are "children" of Wisdom, they are not directly to be identified with her; on the other hand, they do what Wisdom has done by going to

[65]These passages are studied in detail and with specific reference to Q by Felix Christ, *Jesus Sophia. Die Sophia-Christologie bei den Synoptikern*, in: *Abhandlungen zur Theologie des Alten und Neuen Testaments*, 57 (Zurich: Zwingli-Verlag, 1970), pp. 61–154; John Kloppenborg, "Wisdom Christology in Q," *Laval Théologique et Philosophique*, 34 (1978), 129-147; Jacobson, pp. 84-91, 140–143, 183–192, 210–212, and Carlston, pp. 101–106. I am especially indebted to Carlston's analysis in the following paragraphs.

others in the hope of being accepted. Therefore, we may speak of John and Jesus as agents or envoys of Wisdom.

Taken by itself, this passage offers no judgment on the relation of Jesus to John. That must be seen as already answered in the context of Q 15, which clearly recognizes Jesus as the greater of the two.

The wisdom connections of Q 24 are much less obvious but are important in that the "Son" usage here may reflect the influence of wisdom:

> <At that hour Jesus rejoiced in the Spirit>
> and said,
> "I thank you, Father,
>   Lord of heaven and earth,
> that you have hidden these things from the wise and
>   understanding
>   and revealed them to babes.
> Yes, Father,
> for so it was well-pleasing to you.
>
> All things have been delivered to me by my Father;
> and no one knows the Son except the Father,
> no one the Father except the Son
>   and anyone to whom the Son chooses to reveal him."
>
>   Q 24

In the first part of the saying, wisdom tradition may lie behind the Father's revelation to the "babes," for there is a wisdom motif that speaks of human inability to attain it, God's prerogative to give it and God's faithfulness to the simple. In this case, God freely chooses to make known what is hidden from the wise to those who are simple infants, the truly wise.

With regard to the second part of the saying where the Son/Father relationship is spoken of, we may again have the wisdom motif of God alone being the knower of wisdom or of Wisdom making herself known to some. The "Son" title probably stands for "Son of God," and in this wisdom context is best understood as related to a Hellenistic-Jewish

"Son of God" idea that is the masculine counterpart to a "Daughter of God" designation for Wisdom, who knows God intimately and reveals that knowledge to those she seeks out.[66]

In Q 36 we find personified Wisdom herself speaking in a direct quotation. She relates her sending of prophets and apostles and tells of their rejection through persecution and execution:

> Therefore also the wisdom of God said,
> "I will send them prophets and apostles,
> some of whom they will kill and persecute,
> > that the blood of all the prophets
> > which was shed from the foundation of the world
> > may be required (of this generation),
> > > from the blood of Abel to the blood of Zechariah
> > > who perished between the altar and the sanctuary.
> Yes, I tell you,
> it shall be required of this generation."

Q 36 lines 27-35

Wisdom also speaks of the judgment upon those who reject her messengers, namely, "this generation."

At first, this passage may seem to have little to do with a Jesus/Wisdom connection, but Jesus is quoting a saying attributed to Wisdom herself. He does not identify himself with Wisdom who *spoke* the saying (past tense), but there is an obvious connection between what Jesus preaches elsewhere in Q and what Wisdom says here. This Wisdom quotation reinforces what Jesus says about judgment, and his accusations against "this generation" are precisely what Wisdom has predicted here. Therefore, Jesus appears to be once again an agent of Wisdom, yet is not identical with her.

Finally, the lament over Jerusalem (Q 51) is also seen as related to speculative Wisdom traditions. Although the words "wisdom" and "wise" are not used, the contents of

[66]This interpretation of "Son" is suggested by Kloppenborg, pp. 145-146.

this passage so closely resemble the concerns of the previous passage (Q 36 lines 27-35) which quoted Wisdom, that it is probable that this is another quotation from personified Wisdom herself:

> O Jerusalem, Jerusalem,
>   killing the prophets
>   and stoning those who are sent to you!
> How often would I have gathered your children together
>   as a hen gathers her brood under her wings
>   and you would not!
>
> Behold your house is forsaken.
> I tell you, you will not see me until you say,
>   "Blessed is he who comes in the name of the Lord!"
>
> Q 51

Jerusalem, possibly "this generation," has been guilty of rejecting the prophets that Wisdom has sent; she has stoned and killed them and has not responded to Wisdom's offer of protective care. As a result Wisdom declares the forsakenness of Jerusalem's house and will not return until Jerusalem says, "Blessed is he who comes in the name of the Lord!" This reference seems to be to Jesus as the coming judge. What is peculiar about the passage is Jesus speaking in the name of Wisdom, for the identification of Jesus with Wisdom is much closer here than in the other passages we have cited, but he speaks as Wisdom because he is Wisdom's agent or envoy, not because he is identical with her.

When these sayings steeped in the speculative Wisdom tradition are analyzed separately, the relation of Jesus to Wisdom is not crystal clear.[67] In one case, Jesus is portrayed together with John the Baptist as a child of Wisdom, yet carrying on a prophetic mission similar to hers; in another, he is the Father's Son wielding knowledge in the same unique way as Wisdom, the Daughter of God; in another,

[67]Jacobson, p. 230.

Jesus quotes personified Wisdom and thereby preaches what Wisdom says, in effect, acting as Wisdom's agent but without that clear qualification.

The context of Q clarifies the Jesus/John relationship by pointedly saying that Jesus is greater than John (Q 15), and thereafter Q maintains the special position of Jesus as superior to others, though in what way remains ambiguous but special. Therefore, in contrast to Solomon whose wisdom was legendary, Q declares of Jesus, "And behold, something greater than Solomon is here." (Q 34 line 6).

JESUS AS LORD

While Jesus is clearly referred to in Q as the Father's (or God's) Son and while Jesus refers to himself as "son of man," there are amazingly few other designations that are given to him. Although Jesus preaches wisdom, he is never called "Wisdom;" even though his words and deeds reflect the prophet Isaiah's messianic age, Jesus is never identified as the Messiah and the word "Christ" is never applied to him. Clearly bearing the characteristics of a prophet, he is never directly called one. Likewise, Jesus bears a teaching function but is never called "teacher" or "rabbi" directly. The only other designation that Q directly applies to Jesus is "Lord."

The passages that clearly use "Lord" for Jesus and which certainly belong to Q use this designation as a direct address. This occurs always in dialogue (or feigned dialogue) with Jesus and not just in the outer framework of sayings. For instance, in Q 12 (lines 1–2), we find Jesus repeating one of the ways his audience addresses him; the term "Lord" is essential to the saying:

> And why do you call me, "Lord, Lord!"
> and do not do what I tell you?

Also typical is the centurion's words addressed to Jesus:

> Lord, I am not worthy
> to have you come under my roof.

Q 13 lines 9–10

In the mission charge of the disciples, one of them addresses Jesus in this manner:

> Lord, let me first
> go and bury my father.

Q 17 lines 9–10

By itself, this vocative form of address is simply a polite way of speaking, the equivalent of "Sir" in English.[68] As such, it has no special Christological significance. If, on the other hand, it can be shown that other uses of the word "Lord" are applied to Jesus in such a way as to suggest that he is the "Exalted One" who has been raised from the dead, as in the writings of the Apostle Paul, then even these vocative forms of "Lord" may have Christological significance.[69]

The major difficulty in assessing the importance of the remaining passages where "Lord" appears is that there is a basic ambiguity whether the term refers to God (the Father) as it does in the Old Testament or whether it refers to Jesus, as it frequently does in the early church, even when Old Testament passages are quoted.

In our earlier discussion of John the Baptist, we noted the ambiguity of the "Lord" designation in the phrase, "Prepare the way of the Lord" (Q 1 line 5). It seems to refer to God (= Yahweh) whose path toward the end time is being readied by John, but since Jesus comes as the end time judge in the

---

[68]Reginald H. Fuller, "Lord," *Harper's Bible Dictionary* (San Francisco: Harper & Row, Publishers, 1985), p. 573.: "Jesus during his earthly life could be addressed as 'Lord' in recognition of his authority as a teacher (rabbi) and as a charismatic prophet."

[69]Polag, *Die Christologie*, pp. 137, 169–170, holds that "Lord" did have a Christological significance in the later stages of the development of Q traditions, and therefore he conjectures the title of the Q collection to be "The Sayings of the Lord Jesus." This is a questionable conjecture, as the analysis of the Q passages shows.

mind of the Q community, is this Old Testament prophecy being transferred to the person of Jesus who is God's agent of judgment? Likewise, in Q 18 (lines 4–6), we hear of Jesus' admonition to pray to the Lord of the harvest; but who is this "Lord"?

> Pray therefore the Lord of the harvest
> to send out laborers into his harvest.

In the mouth of Jesus, this certainly refers to the Father, because nowhere does Jesus suggest that he be the recipient of prayer. But is this the understanding of the Q community at the time of the final redaction, a community that understands Jesus to be the apocalyptic figure who will gather his own at the judgment (cf. Q 2 lines 12–20)? The "gathering" is a harvest function. This same sort of ambiguity is found in a third important passage, namely Q 51 (line 9): "Blessed is he who comes in the name of the Lord!" Does this mean that Jesus comes in the name of the Father, acting as the Father's agent or as Wisdom's envoy? Certainly on the lips of Jesus, this would be the case, but does this late saying in the Q collection, perhaps, mean that Jesus comes bearing the name of Lord for himself, because he is the resurrected, Exalted One?

The parables of Q in which Jesus makes use of the "Lord" designation are equally difficult to evaluate; cf. Q 47, 54, 75. The first of these speaks of the coming of the master (= lord), the second of a judgment scene in which people say, "Lord, Lord, open to us," and finally a master (= lord) is addressed as "Lord" when he assesses how his servants have used the talents given into their care. These parables are simply stories that speak of "masters" (= lords), but these parabolic stories by their very nature have a function of comparing. In this case, we have a religious situation between the Lord and his people as the point of comparison. But does "Lord" have the connotation of God the Father or Jesus?

This survey of the uses of "Lord" in Q shows that Jesus was addressed as "Lord," but there is no certainty that the word has the technical connotations of the Resurrected One that we find especially in Paul. Most of the Q passages that use the term do not specify whether God (the Father) is meant or Jesus, and often a case can be made for one or the other. If a saying, other than those which use the vocative, is likely to go back to the historical Jesus, it is certainly referring to the Father, since Jesus would hardly speak of himself as the Exalted One before his resurrection. The same cannot be said, however, for the post-Easter Q community which identifies Jesus with the one who is coming to judge, as God's agent in the end time. Given the reluctance of Q to use titles for Jesus, however, and given the fact that none of these sayings requires the application of "Lord" to Jesus as the Exalted One, the Christological significance of "Lord" in Q may be entirely absent.

Spirit in Q

With the exception of one passage (Q 32) which speaks of an "unclean spirit" and "seven other spirits" like it, "Spirit" in all other Q passages of the final redaction refers to something divine. In all cases, then, the word designates a supernatural force that animates humans.

In the case of the unclean spirits, the animating force is demonic and can move in and out of persons and places:

> When the unclean spirit has gone out of someone,
> it passes through waterless places seeking rest
> but finds none;
>   then it says,
>   "I will return to my house from which I came."
> And when it comes, it finds the house swept and put in order.
> Then it goes and brings with itself
>   seven other spirits more evil than itself,
> and they enter and dwell there;
> and the last state of that person is worse than the first.

Q 32

Of particular interest is the second line which speaks of the unclean spirit passing through waterless places seeking rest. Another term for "waterless place" is "desert" or "wilderness," the place where Jesus underwent temptation by the devil and where John preached repentance to his audience. The desert is the place of spiritual combat.

In contrast to this demonic spirit, John the Baptist prophesies about one who is coming who will baptize with the "holy Spirit" and with fire (Q 2 line 16). In the present form, the saying obviously refers to Jesus in the mind of the Q community. While the "fire" clearly is speaking of judgment, is the baptism by Jesus with the holy Spirit referring to the time preceding judgment or is it also a reference to judgment? At an earlier level of Q tradition, the passage was probably contrasting John's baptism with water to a baptism with wind (= spirit) and fire, so that wind and fire both referred to the apocalyptic end time.[70] In the present form of the passage, however, Jesus' baptizing with the holy Spirit only at the end time would be meaningless; what good would it do then? On the other hand, Jesus' baptizing with the holy Spirit, seen in connection with his pre-judgment ministry, would be the way in which his disciples (also the Q prophets) shared in his divine mission, for they would be receiving the same Spirit that animated him as God's prophetic Son.

From the story of his baptism by John, if that material was actually a part of Q, we also learn that Jesus possesses the Spirit:

> And when Jesus had been baptized,
> the heaven was opened
> and the Spirit descended upon him
> <as a dove>.

Q 3 lines 3-4

As Jesus' reception of the Spirit is related here, it clearly has nothing to do with John's baptism, for that was

[70]Jacobson, pp. 33–35.

already past when the heaven opened. The Spirit comes
from heaven, not from John, and this reveals yet another
difference between John and Jesus, for John is not able to
bestow the Spirit on others, whereas John himself indicates
in the passage previously examined (Q 2 lines 12–16) that
the apocalyptic figure of which he speaks "will baptize you
with the holy Spirit and with fire."

The heaven that is opened to allow the Spirit to descend
on Jesus is the same place from which the voice comes
announcing to Jesus, "You are my Son; today I have begot-
ten you" (Q 3 lines 5–7). Since the heavenly voice must
belong to the Father, the implied counterpart to the Son,
then the heavenly Spirit must be understood to be the
Father's Spirit.

This Spirit leads Jesus into the wilderness to be tempted
by the devil (Q 4) and thereby to show the devil, among
other things, how thoroughly Jesus' adoption by God has
taken hold. The Spirit (of God) enables Jesus to speak
authoritatively before the devil himself. And Jesus does this
by quoting God's word to the devil, for he now speaks as
God's prophetic Son. Jesus does not need to study what to
say, nor does he stumble and stammer before coming to an
answer. He speaks with authority because the Spirit of God
animates him. Getting nowhere, the devil leaves, for God is
secure in his prophetic Son who speaks as his agent. There is
no room for further argumentation.

In Q 24, Polag suggests that this important saying which
speaks of Jesus' interpretation of the Father/Son relationship began possibly with these words: "<At that hour Jesus
rejoiced in the Spirit> and said..." (lines 1–2). While this
wording is uncertain, it is in keeping with the picture of
Jesus in the temptation story. Jesus speaks authoritatively
about his special relation to the Father, because he possesses
the Father's Spirit. He is only making known the Father's
understanding, because the Father is speaking through him
by means of his Spirit.

Yet another definition of the relationship of Jesus to the
Spirit becomes apparent in the saying of Q 40:

> And whoever says a word against the son of man
>   will be forgiven;
> but whoever blasphemes against the holy Spirit
>   will not be forgiven.

Q 40

It is important in this passage to understand the term "son of man" as Jesus' way of saying "me," and we must not see any sort of apocalyptic authority standing behind the son of man terminology here or we will miss the point of the passage. Jesus as an ordinary human being can be spoken against and those who do so can be forgiven for that, just as any other person can be spoken against and the speakers can be forgiven by God; the difference occurs when the holy Spirit becomes involved, because to speak against the holy Spirit is blasphemy, for the Spirit is divine, coming from God, the Father. In other words, humans can be forgiven for speaking against other people, including the person of Jesus, but no one may be forgiven who blasphemes against God himself.[71] This passage implies the very human origins of Jesus that we noted in discussion of the meaning of his baptism by John and before his adoption by God.

This interpretation may seem, at first, to contradict the words of Q 39:

> But I tell you,
> every one who acknowledges me before others,
>   the son of man also will acknowledge before the angels
>   of God;
>
> but whoever denies me before others
>   will be denied before the angels of God.

Q 39

The crucial issue in this passage is what is meant by acknowledging or denying Jesus. Certainly the point here is not confessing or denying Jesus as a human being but as

---

[71]Jacobson, p. 229: "...the messenger is one thing, that which comes to expression through him another."

God's prophetic Son, the possessor of the heavenly Spirit.[72] In Q 40 a distinction was being made between the person of Jesus and the heavenly Spirit that has come to him, but in this passage of Q 39 such a distinction is not being made; rather, Jesus is understood in this latter case to be God's spokesman, the one possessing God's Spirit. This passage stresses the unity of the Spirit with Jesus, the other emphasizes their separateness from one another. It is a difference, then, of perspective, but not necessarily a case of contradiction.

The last passage to speak directly of the Spirit (again a disputed wording!) is Q 41 which refers to the disciples of Jesus and, therefore, also to the Q prophets:

> And when they bring you before the synagogues
> <and the councils>
> do not be anxious how or what you are to say;
> for the holy Spirit will teach you in that very hour
> what you are to say.

Q 41

Here we find the disciples of Jesus in a position similar to what Jesus was facing in the wilderness when being tempted by the devil (Q 4). Even as Jesus who possessed the Spirit did not need to worry about what to say to the devil, because the Spirit enabled him to speak to the devil authoritatively, so also the disciples of Jesus need to have no fear concerning what to say when haled before synagogues and councils, because they possess the same divine Spirit as Jesus and that same Spirit will instruct them what to say in that troubled situation. In other words, they will speak authoritatively too, for in their understanding they have been "baptized with the holy Spirit" by Jesus, as John the Baptist had prophesied (Q 2).

Q is silent about the role of the Spirit in connection with

---

[72]One could possibly interpret this passage in the sense of Jesus being Wisdom's agent. To reject Jesus who speaks in Wisdom's stead is to reject God who speaks through Wisdom. In this case, the unity of Wisdom with Jesus is being emphasized.

the specific charismatic gifts of healing, exorcising, raising the dead, judging and preaching, unless the last named was implied in speaking before synagogues and councils. But this does not mean that these are not spiritual gifts, for Jesus does all these things after having received the heavenly Spirit. His entire ministry must be understood as a manifestation of the Spirit. Likewise, his disciples who continue his prophetic ministry and who possess this same Spirit are, in fact, exercising spiritual gifts just as Jesus did. Therefore, despite the relatively few references to the Spirit in Q, the Spirit plays a decisive role in Q theology.

The Q Community and Its Mission

The traditions and sayings of Q arose and were preserved in a social context.[73] These sayings must have had both speakers and hearers, and so there is a social dimension to this material by the very fact that it exists. When we examine the Q sayings, it seems an inescapable conclusion that at least the earliest of them must have gone back to Jesus himself; they are grounded in the ministry of the historical Jesus. The reason his sayings were preserved is that his message must have struck responsive chords in the ears and hearts of those who first heard them. As such, they were remembered and because of the peculiar qualities of what was heard and remembered, the sayings were retold and passed on to others, most likely family, friends, and close associates of other sorts.

It must be presupposed that those sayings that most intimately touched their audiences because of their social relevancy and acceptability were assured of survival. That is not to say, however, that only those sayings were preserved which were not alien or offensive to those who heard them, because odd or unusual statements can be remembered and

[73]These comments on the nature of the Q community are greatly indebted to the insights of Kelber, pp. 24–26, who is, in turn, commenting on and expanding beyond the suggestions of Gerd Theissen, *Sociology of Early Palestinian Christianity*, trans. John Bowden (Philadelphia: Fortress Press, 1978).

passed on precisely because of their peculiarity. Generally, however, the oral transmission is controlled by what Kelber calls the "law of social identification" of the audience with the message, rather than by the technique of verbatim memorization,[74] though there was undoubtedly some of that as well.

This observation about social identification raises some intriguing questions concerning the nature of the Q community, especially in the earlier stages of its existence, because there are a number of sayings in Q that betray some rather unusual characteristics that might cause them to be termed "antisocial sayings." These sayings offend some deeply held convictions about the importance of a home, family loyalty and responsiblity, and a respect for and pride in property and wealth.[75] Most, but not all, of these sayings occur in the section of Q that Polag has entitled "Mission of the Disciples" (Q 17–28).

The first saying about the disciples' mission contains no less than three antisocial sayings:

> And <along the road> someone said to him,
> "I will follow you wherever you go."
> And Jesus said to that person,
> "Foxes have holes,
>   and birds of the air have nests;
> but the son of man no-
>   where to lay his head."

> But another said to him,
> "Lord, let me first
> go and bury my father."
> But Jesus said to that person,
> "Follow me,
> and leave the dead to bury their own dead."

> But another said,
> "I will follow you, Lord;

---

[74]Kelber, p. 24. His reluctance to admit little or no verbatim memorization seems exaggerated.

[75]Kelber, p. 24.

> but let me first
> say farewell to those at my home."
> But Jesus said to that person,
> "No one who puts a hand to the plow
> and looks back
> is fit for the kingdom of God."

Q 17

The first hard saying requires homelessness of the person who chooses to follow Jesus, for unlike even the animals, Jesus and his followers have no place to sleep, no home. The second saying offends nearly all sensitivity, for the radical call of Jesus requires such an immediate and total response that even burial of one's own father is not permitted. The third saying, which may or may not belong to Q since it appears only in the special Lucan material, is no less offensive, because the follower of Jesus is not allowed to say good-bye to those at home, to the family.

The family relationship comes in for another jolt in Q 58, where it is required of Jesus' followers to hate the members of their families:[76]

> If any one comes to me
> and does not hate father and mother
> and son and daughter,
> that one cannot be my disciple.

Q 58 lines 1–4

Nor does hospitality, which was ordinarily a grave obligation, escape excision:

[76]Cf. Q 48 lines 5–11 which speak of divisions within families caused by Jesus who has come not to bring peace but a sword:

> Do you think that I have come to bring peace on earth?
> I tell you, not peace but a sword.
> For in one house five will be divided,
> three against two and two against three | they will be divided,
> father against son and son against father,
> mother against daughter and daughter against mother,
> mother-in-law against her daughter-in-law and daughter-in-law
> against mother-in-law.

> Carry no purse, no bag, no sandals;
> and salute no one on the road

Q 21 lines 1–2

The follower of Jesus is told not to greet anyone on the way from one place to another. This passage is important also for the place of personal wealth and goods of the followers. They are to carry no purse and, therefore, have no money; they have no bag and, therefore, have no possessions, not even other clothes to bring along with them; they wear no sandals and, therefore, have no protection for their feet as they travel from one place to another.

Having just seen the radically offensive nature of these sayings, we might well ask what kind of people would listen to, accept, remember, and pass these sayings on. Who would continue to hold to such sayings and why would sayings like these be transmitted to others? What social conditions would lead to the transmission of such an antisocial message?[77]

If it is accurate that those sayings which are preserved and passed on are normally those which have been sympathetically received by an audience, then we must be speaking about an audience that stood on the fringe of its society, people whose experience as outsiders predisposed them to be interested in a message that called for acceptance of poverty, homelessness, rejection and sundering of family relationships and entailing a life on the road. This fringe group was itself unsettled and, no doubt, also unsettling to the rest of society. They accepted this antisocial message, remembered it and passed it on to others because it rang true to their own experience.[78]

From a survey of the Q sayings, we can define this early audience as early Christian itinerant prophets, charismatics who were homeless, unpropertied, and who considered themselves to be loyal followers of Jesus, adopting his

[77]Kelber, p. 24.
[78]Kelber, p. 24.

mobile manner of life and accepting his words that lent support to it.[79] They so identified their lives with his, that they could also speak for him. The prophetic figure of Jesus, who stands himself in line with the prophets of Israel and who is understood to be the prophet par excellence by the Q community, is emulated by the Q prophets who continue to speak his words of the past as well as his words in the present, for they believed that Jesus was present in their message and speaking through them. This self-understanding of the Q prophets is underscored in Q 23 which speaks of the relation of Jesus to his followers:

> Whoever hears you hears me,
> and whoever rejects you rejects me;
> and whoever rejects me rejects him who sent me.

Q 23

As this passage indicates, there have been some who have listened to their message and accepted it; others who have rejected it. Acceptance of this message includes acceptance of the suffering of Jesus but not an imitation of his death; rather, they experience the rejection and the possibility of death that was the common fate of prophets, in whose community they stand:

> Blessed are you when (people) hate you
> and exclude and revile you
> and utter evil against you
> on account of the son of man.
> Rejoice and be glad,

[79]Richard Dillon, "Early Christian Experience in the Gospel Sayings," *The Bible Today*, 21 (1983), 86, raises a *caveat* about too readily seeing the situation of the Q community as a reflection of that of the historical Jesus: "Several pronouncements in the mission instruction [of Q] reflect circumstances which are not easily located in Jesus' earthly ministry. These include the persecution of his disciples (Luke 10:3), the imposition of a severely ascetical life style (10:4; contrast Mark 2:19–20 and Luke 7:34), and the rejection of Jesus by towns either not mentioned elsewhere (Luke 10:13) or else mentioned as theaters of successful ministry (10:15)."

> for your reward is great in heaven:
> for so their ancestors did to the prophets.

Q 5 lines 10–16

The strong theme of rejection in Q confirms that these rootless followers of Jesus were suspect to the rest of settled society. They were perceived by settled society as beggars and vagrants; they suffered hunger and thirst, loneliness, and persecution.[80]

Having identified at least one part of the Q community as itinerant charismatic prophets who were on the move proclaiming Jesus' words, can we also identify who their audience was and who it was that rejected their message? The earlier stages of Q material point to an answer that coincides with Jesus' own audience, namely, his fellow Jews. The mission of Jesus was to the Jews, and the early Q community continued that mission work, even as it continued Jesus' message.

Already the preaching of John the Baptist is done before a Jewish audience. The "brood of vipers" that he addresses are admonished to bear fruit that befits repentance and not rely on their historical association with Israel to carry them through judgment:

> And do not begin to say to yourselves,
>   "We have Abraham as our father;"
> for I tell you that God is able
>   from these stones to raise up children
>   to Abraham.

Q 2 lines 5–8

Jesus' sermon on the mount presumes a Jewish audience too. The reference to the prophets in Q 5 line 16 is to the prophets of Israel whose ancestors excluded and reviled them. Also the comparison made in Q 6 reflects a Jewish audience:

[80]Kelber, pp. 24–25.

And if you salute your own,
  what reward have you?
Do not even Gentiles do the same?

Q 6 lines 17–19

The Gentiles are contrasted with the audience that Jesus is addressing. In other passages the term that comes to the fore for the Jewish audience that rejects Jesus and his message is "this generation" (Q 16 line 1). It is this audience that attacks Jesus for being "a glutton and a drunkard, a friend of tax collectors and sinners." Since tax collectors often were Jewish collaborators with the Romans and, therefore, hated by Jews as traitors, the reproach against Jesus here can only be understood as coming from a Jewish audience.[81]

If Polag is correct in including Q 20 among the sayings of Q (It appears only in Matthew 10:5b.), then we have a clear setting of the parameters of the mission:

(Go nowhere among the Gentiles,
  and enter no town of the Samaritans,
  but go rather to the lost sheep of the house of Israel.)

Q 20

This corresponds with another passage found only in Matthew 10:23 which Polag also conjectures was part of Q:

[When they persecute you in one town,
  flee to the next;

---

[81] Paul Hoffmann, "Die Anfänge der Theologie in der Logienquelle," in: *Gestalt und Anspruch des Neuen Testaments*, ed. Josef Schreiner and Gerhard Dautzenberg (Würzburg: Echter-Verlag, 1969), pp. 147-151, interprets "this generation" and its opposition to the Q community in terms of the politico-religious situation in Palestine at the time. According to him, Jewish nationalists (insurrectionists) were seeking support for their military goals of political salvation at the same time that the Q community with its emphasis on the demand for goodness, love of enemies, mercifulness, and the forbiddance of judging others was seeking recruits for its entirely different understanding of salvation. This led inevitably to conflict between the two groups, with the result that the Q prophets were rejected by "this generation."

truly , I say to you,
you will not have gone through all the towns of Israel
   before the son of man comes.]

Q 42

Numerous other passages from Q indicate a Jewish audience, such as Q 60 which speaks of work on the Sabbath, Q 62 which refers to the law and prophets, that is, Jewish scriptures, and Q 63 that underscores the validity of the law. Another contrast with Gentiles is made in this passage:

And do not be anxious saying,
   "What shall we eat?" or "What shall we drink?" or
   "What shall we wear?"
For the Gentiles seek all these things.

Q 43 lines 23–25

The Q prophets expect to be brought before "synagogues and <councils>" (Q 41 line 1); the prophets and kings of Israel are referred to in Q 25 line 3; Jesus speaks the brooding words of Wisdom over Jerusalem in Q 51, and God is addressed in a Jewish manner in the Lord's Prayer (Q 26).

The rejection of the Q community's message and its prophets, including Jesus, leads to the hostility on the part of the community apparent in the "brood of vipers" language attributed to John the Baptist and the derisive "this generation" attributed to Jesus. This proceeds a step further, of course, to include the threat of judgment and rejection by God, but it also opens up the possibility of a mission to the Gentiles.

In a passage that bristles with condemnation, while speaking of the fate of the prophets, the woes leveled against the lawyers and the Pharisees are broadened to include "this generation:"

Therefore also the wisdom of God said,
"I will send them prophets and apostles,

some of whom they will kill and persecute,
> that the blood of all the prophets
> which was shed from the foundation of the world
> may be required (of this generation),
>> from the blood of Abel to the blood of Zechariah
>> who perished between the altar and the sanctuary.
> Yes, I tell you,
> it shall be required of this generation."

Q 36 lines 27–35

This appears to be a later addition to the Q sayings, since it speaks directly of Wisdom (and possibly of apostles) and may reflect the community's knowledge of the deaths of John the Baptist and of Jesus.

In a pair of sayings related to one another, "this generation" is described as an evil generation, seeking a sign:

> "This generation is an evil generation;
> it seeks a sign, but no sign shall be given to it
> except the sign of Jonah.
>
> For as Jonah became a sign to the people of Nineveh,
> so will the son of man be to this generation."

Q 33 lines 4–8

Contrary to many interpretations of this passage, son of man is not an apocalyptic figure here, and the reference is not to future judgment at the end time but to a present situation.[82] As Jonah, a prophet of repentance, became a sign to the people of Nineveh, a wicked Gentile city, so will Jesus, as a prophet of repentance be a sign to this generation, his Jewish audience. Nothing is said about the response of that audience yet. In the following Q passage, however, it is clear that "this generation" has not given the proper response to Jesus. It has not responded to Jesus as the Ninevites had listened to Jonah, so it stands condemned.

---

[82]So Meyer, p. 409.

Both the queen of the south and the people of Nineveh condemn "this generation." This is significant because at least the Ninevites and perhaps also the queen are Gentiles. The Gentiles have responded when the Jews (=this generation) have rejected the prophetic message sent to them by God. Here we see the bridge to the Gentile mission which seems to have become an essential part of the later Q community's task.

It is the impenitence of the Jewish audience, the rejection of Jesus' message that led to the mission to the Gentiles, and it is the acceptance of the message by the Gentiles that leads them, in turn, to condemn the unbelieving Jewish audience for their lack of response. Behind these Jonah sayings lies the hope that the unbelieving Jews will be shamed into repentance and into following Jesus, taking note of Jonah's sign and the Gentile response to his message. This is important, for in Jesus is to be found someone greater than Solomon and Jonah.[83]

A similar reproach to the Jewish audience of the Q preaching is found in the miracle story of the healing of the centurion's servant. As we noted earlier, this story is less concerned with the healing than with the dialogue of Jesus with the centurion. In that discussion, the Gentile centurion's faith in Jesus' power to heal his servant is so strong and his humility so great that he declares to Jesus:

> Lord, I am not worthy
> to have you come under my roof;
> but say the word, and my servant will be healed.

Q 13 lines 9–11

The centurion recognizes the authority of Jesus, and Jesus is said to have marveled and declared to his followers:

[83]Meyer, pp. 406–410.

> [Truly], I say to you,
> not even in Israel have I found such faith.

> Q 13 lines 19–20

What has taken place is that the faith of a Gentile has been praised over against the response of Israel. A rebuke to Israel is implied in this contrast of belief. It is a way of shaming Israel into making the proper response, into following the example of the Gentile centurion's faith. The other side of the issue is also apparent: the Q community has accepted the mission to the Gentiles, and this is underscored by having Jesus speak in such glowing terms with and about a Gentile.[84]

Two passages of Q use the banquet theme and both of them address the issues of Gentile acceptance of the kingdom of God, Jewish rejection of it and the ensuing consequence of condemnation.

In the first of these, the eschatological banquet is described in which Gentiles (= those from the east and west) will sit at the table with the patriarchs of Israel and all the prophets in the kingdom of God.[85] Inclusion in the kingdom is not based at all on physical descendance from Israel, because the Gentiles' presence contrasts with the situation of the unbelieving Jews, of whom it is said:

> But you will be thrown into the outer darkness.
> There people will weep and gnash their teeth.

> Q 55 lines 5–6

As we noted earlier, John the Baptist's preaching to the "brood of vipers" also rejected special consideration based on physical descendance from Israel, though there was nothing that directly implies the shift to the Gentiles in his preaching; cf. Q 2.[86]

---

[84]Meyer, pp. 410–411.

[85]Some point out that the future tense in this passage of Q indicates that there was no mission to the Gentiles as yet.

[86]Meyer, pp. 411–412.

The second of the banquet passages appears in the form of a parable:

> A man gave a great banquet
>> and invited many,
> and sent his servant to say to those who had been
>> invited,
>> "Come; for all is now ready,"
> but they would not come.
> . . .
>> and the servant reported this to his master.
> Then the householder in anger said to his servant,
>> "Go out into the thoroughfares,
>> and compel people to come in."
> And the house was filled with guests.
> I tell you,
>> none of those invited shall taste my banquet.

Q 57

This parable provides a reason for the mission to the Gentiles. The Jews were the first to be invited, but they have refused to come. In the wake of their refusal to respond to God's invitation to come and to have a share in the kingdom, the invitation has now been given to outsiders, that is, to the Gentiles. Furthermore, the passage makes it clear that God (= the master) has willed the inclusion of the Gentiles. The privileged position of Israel has ended with the refusal to accept the invitation that was first made to them.[87]

In the previous passage, the servant who delivered the master's invitation was probably a reference to divine Wisdom (and by extension, Jesus who speaks that wisdom); in the lament over Jerusalem (Q 51), we again find Wisdom bemoaning the response of Israel to God's message. The prophets that have been sent to Israel have been stoned and killed, and Wisdom's motherly wings that provide warmth and protection have been spurned. As a result Israel itself

---

[87]Meyer, pp. 412–415.

has been forsaken. The door has not yet been closed, but Wisdom will not return till welcomed in the name of the Lord.[88]

What therefore began solely as a mission to the Jews in the ministry of Jesus and the early stages of the Q community seems to have expanded to the Gentiles after the rejection of the message by the Jewish audience. Little hope seems to be expressed in the extant Q sayings of a major shift in Jewish attitudes that would signal repentance and acceptance of the kingdom of God, as it has been manifested in the person of Jesus. They have denied what is essential for entrance into that kingdom, and physical descendance from Israel is no guarantee for acceptance into the kingdom. Gentiles and Jews have the same requirements and both may still enter, but Q points out the serious consequences to the Jews who have refused God's invitation; it will mean exclusion from the future kingdom unless the impenitence is removed.[89] The reason for the emphasis on the Jews is that it is among the Jews where the ministry of Jesus and the early Q community had its locus.

One further note about the Gentiles is important to keep in mind. When Q speaks of acceptance of Gentiles, there is no indication that the acceptance is perceived in the Pauline sense. The Q community remains a community of Christian-Jews who continue their Jewish practices; therefore, for a Gentile convert to become a member of the Q community probably meant becoming, in effect, a Christian-Jew, following the Jewish law and customs like the rest of the community. It is precisely this kind of Gentile mission that Paul was adamantly opposed to but one which the Q community could hardly have conceived of in any other way.

Even as there was a shift in the later Q community from the Jewish to the Gentile mission, so there was a change in the composition and nature of the Q community itself much earlier. The original group of itinerant charismatic prophets

[88]Meyer, pp. 415–417.
[89]Meyer, p. 417.

hardly seems like the kind of people that would be interested in writing down the sayings of Jesus. They were living them out quite literally and needed no reminders of what Jesus had to say, so it is doubtful that these prophets were the exclusive bearers of the antisocial message of the prophets; indeed, the antisocial character of some of the sayings make it difficult to conceive of a Q community at all unless other dynamics were present besides those provided by the charismatic itinerants. As Kelber notes, "Experience teaches us that one can well remember and reproduce information without living out its content in one's personal life."[90] Such a viewpoint may have been held by audiences more settled in society than the Q prophets. They could identify with these sayings as a matter of principle but not live them out literally. In other words, the social identification is not necessarily limited to one specific group.

The composition of Q may have been undertaken by a more settled audience than the Q prophets, and the number of scholarly works that deal with stages of development of the Q document support the view that Q was not a static repository of the sayings of Jesus and of the early Q prophets. Instead, it was a body of material that grew and developed. If the Q movement was to grow, a more broadly based audience was necessary than that supplied by the Q prophets.[91] That is what, in fact, happened.

Epilogue

Our look at various important elements of Q theology does not mean that we have been speaking of *the* Q theology. The reason for backing away from such a claim is that as the Q community developed, it added new ideas and expanded upon old ones, so that there is not always a perfect consistency of thought in the theological perspectives (e.g., John the Baptist and Jesus are seen as equal in Q 16, both

[90]Kelber, p. 25.
[91]Kelber, p. 26.

being children of Wisdom, whereas Jesus is portrayed as superior to John in almost all other Q passages that speak of the relation between the two.).

The recognition of various layers of Q tradition has led to a number of studies that have tried to delineate the stages of development of Q thought. The results of such efforts have not led to uniformity of opinion among scholars, although the basic methodological procedure is now widely accepted. There is a danger, of course, that too much weight is placed on development of concepts that we know too little about, so that widely divergent viewpoints result (e.g., Tödt's understanding of Jesus' use of "Son of Man" and Vermes' understanding of Jesus' use of "son of man" end in entirely different reconstructions of the earliest level of Q thought). Another problem that arises is that such studies attempt to show how the text of Q, as used by Matthew and Luke, came to be but stop short of taking that final redaction of Q seriously as a text in itself. It is a classic case of looking at the trees but failing to see the forest.

The other side of this issue is also not without its problems. Once inconsistencies have been noted, they simply cannot be ignored; otherwise, harmonization of differing viewpoints results in distortion and oversimplification. That is to look at the forest without noting the variety of the trees that the forest consists of.

Our study has tried to look at Q primarily in the form that Matthew and Luke have preserved it, while taking note of some of the development of ideas which help to explain this final redaction. Even though we may not speak of *the* Q theology, there are elements that seem fairly consistent in Q thought (e.g., God in Q). The understanding of the person and role of Jesus, on the other hand, certainly underwent significant development from the historical Jesus to the Jesus who is the prophetic Son of God and agent of divine Wisdom. Some differences, such as the mission only to the house of Israel becoming in the final stages of Q a mission also to the Gentiles, are important, to be sure, but must not be overdrawn; the Gentiles, who were invited, were, no doubt, accepted only as converts to this Christian-Jewish sect in the sense of becoming proselytes in the usual Jewish understanding. This can hardly be compared to the trauma that Paul's understanding of the Gentile mission must have had upon such Christian-Jewish communities as Q.

One area that was not often touched on in our discussion is that of recovering the genuine sayings of the historical Jesus. It was precisely this concern that originally attracted scholars to the study of Q, but this interest has subsided in more recent studies, as we have come to realize that the Q community did not make a distinction between the historical Jesus and the Jesus alive in the voice of the Q prophets who spoke in his name.[92] Untangling the Q prophets from the historical Jesus is no easy task, and the results have been far from unanimous scholarly opinion. There has been a definite shift away from trying to recover the "very words" (*ipsissima verba*) of the historical Jesus to a less precise "very voice" (*ipsissima vox*) of the historical Jesus, that is, the type of material rather than the precise wording that may have come from Jesus during his earthly existence. Undoubtedly Q has some of the latter and, perhaps, also some of the former, but this material is embedded in a theological document, Q, which has its own way of looking at the person and role of Jesus, as he continues to speak to the Q community. Q offers no easy entry to solving the problem of the historical Jesus.

Of all the features of Q, perhaps, the most striking to the modern reader is its lack of material on the meaning of Jesus' death. The Q community was a group of Christian-Jews who know of Jesus' death but attached no redemptive significance to it. The primary saving event is seen, rather, in the future, an event which will take place soon when Jesus returns for judgment. Even though the resurrection of Jesus is never mentioned in Q, it is the presupposition for connecting the historical Jesus who died with the Jesus who will come as judge. That such a perspective did not gain precedence in later Christian thought does not mean that it was unknown elsewhere. Even Paul seems to be aware of this

[92]Zeller, pp. 11–14.

theology in 1 Thessalonians 1:9-10, a formulaic construc-
tion that faithfully summarizes some of the key teaching of
Q theology, including the presupposition of the resurrection.[93] It is a theology that he did not develop in his own
letters and one which later conflicted with his missionary
goals among the Gentiles:

> ...and how you turned to God
>   from idols
>   to serve a living and true God
>   and to wait for his Son from heaven
>   whom he raised from the dead, Jesus
>   who delivers us from the wrath to come.

1 Thess. 1:9b-10 (RSV)

---

[93]Ivan Havener, "The Pre-Pauline Christological Credal Formulae of 1 Thessalonians," *Society of Biblical Literature Seminar Papers Series*, 20. ed. Kent
Harold Richards (Chico, CA: Scholars Press, 1981), pp. 105–110, espec. 109–110.

PART TWO

The Text of Q
by
Athanasius Polag

Preface

At the present time, literary-critical attempts to reconstruct Q are treated on the whole with considerable reserve. Be that as it may, it must be admitted that research into the redaction of the Gospels has greatly extended our knowledge of the methods used by the redactors of Matthew and Luke in their handling of the texts transmitted to them. Where the methods of form-criticism are used to evaluate the findings of literary-critical research, it is often possible to say that one form of the text is primary, the other secondary. As a result, various scholars have made renewed attempts to ascertain what the original text of individual sayings was by comparing the texts of the sayings in Matthew and Luke and to refer to this original text in their interpretation of the sayings transmitted by Matthew and Luke. A certain convergence of opinion can be observed among scholars who have made such attempts. This textbook is a contribution to this field of scholarship. Its aim is not, as one might suppose, to reconstruct Q as a whole, nor to ascertain with the maximum degree of certainty the content of Q. It offers merely a reconstruction of the text of the common ancestor of Matthew and Luke in the last stage of transmission.

It is not possible within the limits of a textbook to give the reasons why one form of the text is accepted as older than another. The arguments in support of the choice between variants can be examined in the relevant literature. The student using this literature should bear three points in mind. First it must be said in general that to follow the majority of scholars in choosing between variants is not always the better course. Scholars have, unfortunately, too often taken over opinions of their predecessors, without having tested those opinions for accuracy. Furthermore, not all the sayings have attracted the same amount of attention in scholarly research; certain scholars have ventured an opinion about only a small number of sayings. Further difficulties arise through the fact that some scholars have shown a one-sided preference for Matthew or Luke. This is true, for example, of Adolf Harnack and his followers, who make too sweeping generalizations in their judgment of the reliability of Matthew's version. On the other side, certain scholars in the English-speaking world and Heinz Schürmann in Germany are rightly criticised for their preference for Luke. In many cases Rudolf Bultmann bases his choice of a particular variant on general form-critical considerations but fails to take the circumstances of transmission in a particular case sufficiently into account.

This book offers a working text which attempts to provide a bird's eye view of material that requires elaborate analyses, if it is to be worked through in detail. It tries to show what possibilities still exist for the reconstruction of the Q version of the sayings transmitted in Matthew and Luke. In the present state of research it is not enough just to print the parallel texts in juxtaposition as in a synopsis, nor is it sufficient to try to reconstruct the common ancestor of Matthew and Luke in the case of individual sayings. This book tries to overcome these deficiencies. Q is an important branch of the Jesus-tradition. If students are to be encouraged to analyze the text for themselves, they must be provided with adequate material from which they can work.

The Text

The method used here for presenting those texts of Q capable of reconstruction is the one that has become general practice in the editing of fragmentary patristic texts. In establishing the text, the following principles have been observed, in order to take into account the special circumstances of the transmission of individual texts:

In cases where the texts of Matthew and Luke differ, the version that appears to be the original, according to literary-critical and redaction-critical standards, is printed in the body of the text.

Those parts of the transmitted material which are given by both Matthew and Luke but in versions that are not equivalent or identical, appear in italics. In cases where the material is identical or where the difference is merely one of word endings or between a word and its compound, bold print is used.

Those parts of the text for which there is a high degree of likelihood that they had an archetype in Q are given in brackets. The brackets indicate the degree of probability as follows:

> (...) probability
> [...] conjecture
> <...> possibility

At certain points it can reasonably be claimed on the grounds of characteristically Matthaean or Lucan language, that neither of the two forms reproduces the original text. In such cases that version is admitted, as a rule, which offers us the original text in the remaining part of the saying. Only in a very small number of places in the text is an omission marked by a series of dots. This means that no reasonably certain conclusion could be drawn about the priority of one or the other of the variants.

The text is divided into numbered lines.

Chapter and verse numbers of the parallel passages in Matthew and Luke are given in the left or right margins, respectively. In cases where the verse division is different in Matthew and Luke, the difference is indicated in the text by a vertical line.

Each saying is numbered, even where it forms part of a larger group of sayings. Where a number of short sayings, however, form a small group, only one number is used. The same applies to cases where short sayings are added at the end of a group. Words providing a framework for, or introduction to a saying are treated as part of the saying which they introduce, even in cases where the introductory words apply to more than one saying in a group. In cases where it can be assumed that a saying appeared in Q, but where the text cannot be reconstituted (it appears in italics and in brackets), the saying is nevertheless included in the numbering.

For the sequence of sayings, the order of Luke is generally preferred. The larger group of sayings are introduced by a capital letter and a heading.

Where there are only a few indications that a saying appeared in Q, the saying is printed in Appendix I. Such a saying is numbered according to its place in the sequence of the main text, but with a letter of the alphabet added, e.g. 39a. In these cases, as well as in those where the saying probably appeared in Q, an attempt is made to show what occurred at the redaction stage. What may be suspected to be redactional only is enclosed in < >.

Appendix II lists those words that provide a framework or introduction to a saying and that can only with considerable reserve be regarded as having appeared in Q. They are given only by Luke and for the most part appear in the second part of the collection. The sayings introduced by these words in Luke always appear in a variant form in Matthew. It can reasonably be assumed that the Matthew redactor dropped the introductory words because they were inappropriate to his version.

Passages of Mark whose content corresponds to passages transmitted in Q appear in Appendix III. To facilitate comparison they are printed according to the sequence of Q. A complete overview of these parallel passages is also given.

For scriptural quotations within Q, the corresponding texts of the Septuagint (LXX) are given in Appendix IV, so that the divergences can easily be noted.

Trier, Summer 1978   Athanasius Polag

Translator's Note

Wherever possible I have tried to follow the English of the Revised Standard Version of the New Testament and Launcelot Lee Brenton's translation of the Septuagint texts. At times, however, more precision was necessary in order to preserve the peculiarities of the Greek texts, and there was a pressing need to remove unnecessarily sexist language; in those instances, I have altered the existing translations. The extensive critical apparatus to Fr. Polag's Greek text of the Q fragments has been entirely omitted in this translation. *

Ivan Havener

* *Original Title*: Polag, Athanasius. *Fragmenta Q. Textheft zur Logienquelle.* Neukirchen-Vluyn: Neukirchener Verlag, 1979. Second edition with corrections, 1982.

Table of Q Contents

No.		Matt.	Luke	Page
A. Introduction				
1	[Arrival of the Baptist]	3:1–3	3:2b–4	123
2	Preaching of Repentance/			
	Abraham's Descendants	3:7–10	3:7–9	123
	The Coming One/			
	Spirit Baptism	3:11, 12	3:16, 17	123
3	[Baptism of Jesus]	4:13, 16	3:21b, 22	124
4	Temptation of Jesus	4:1–11	4:1–13	124
B. Sermon on the Mount				
5	Introduction	5:1,2	6:12, 20a	125
	Beatitudes	5:3–10	6:20b, 21	125
	Beatitude of			
	the Persecuted	5:11, 12	6:22, 23	125
6	Love of One's Enemies	5:44	6:27, 28	125
	Patience	5:39b–41	6:29	125
	Giving and Lending	5:42	6:30	125
	Decisive Behavior	5:45–47	6:32–35	125
7	Merciful Like the Father	5:48	6:36	126
	Judging/Giving/			
	Measuring	7:1, 2	6:37,38	126
8	Golden Rule	7:12	6:31	126
9	Blind Leaders	15:14	6:39	126
	Disciple and Teacher	10:24, 25	6:40	126

No.		Matt.	Luke	Page
10	Log and Speck	7:3–5	6:41, 42	126
11	Good and Bad Tree	7:16–20	6:43, 44	127
	Heart's Treasure	12:34b, 35	6:45	127
12	"Lord, Lord!" Sayer	7:21	6:46	127
	House Construction	7:24–27	6:47–49	127
13	Conclusion and Transition	7:28	7:1a	127
	Centurion of Capernaum	8:5–10, 13	7:1b–10	127

C. John the Baptist

14	The Baptist's Question	11:2, 3	7:18–20	128
	Answer to the Question	11:4–6	7:22, 23	128
15	Witness to the Baptist	11:7–9	7:24–26	128
	Quotation from Mal. 3:1	11:10	7:27	128
	The One Who Is Greater	11:11	7:28	128
16	The Obstinate Children	11:16–19	7:31–35	129

D. Mission of the Disciples

17	Discipleship—"Foxes"	8:19, 20	9:57, 58	129
	Discipleship—"Burial of the Dead"	8:21, 22	9:59, 60	129
	Discipleship—"Looking Back"	—	9:61, 62	129
18	<Appointment and Mission>	9:37a	10:1, 2a	130
	Plentiful Harvest and Few Laborers	9:37, 38	10:2b	130
19	Like Sheep among Wolves	10:16a	10:3	130
20	(To the Scattered of Israel)	10:5b, 6	—	130
21	Conduct on the Way	10:9–13	10:4–7	130
	Conduct in Town	10:7–15	10:8–12	130
22	Woes to the Towns	11:21–23	10:13–15	131
23	The Authority of the Mission	10:40	10:16	131
24	Prayer of Joy	11:25–27	10:21, 22	131
25	Beatitude of the Eye-witnesses	13:16, 17	10:23, 24	131

No.		Matt.	Luke	Page
	E. On Prayer			
26	Lord's Prayer	6:9–13	11:2–4	132
27	Answering of Prayer	7:7, 8	11:9, 10	132
28	Asking the Father	7:9–11	11:11–13	132
	F. Controversies			
29	Beelzebul Name Calling	12:22–24	11:14, 15	132
	Answer 1: Kingdom of Satan	12:25, 26	11:17, 18	133
	Answer 2: Kingdom of God	12:27, 28	11:19, 20	133
30	The Stronger	12:29	11:21, 22	133
31	For and Against Jesus	12:30	11:23	133
32	Relapse	12:43–45	11:24–26	133
33	Demand for Signs/ Sign of Jonah	12:38, 39	11:16, 29	134
	Interpretative Saying	12:40	11:30	134
34	Queen of the South/ Ninevites	12:41, 42	11:31, 32	134
35	Lamp on a Stand	5:15	11:33	134
	On the Eye	6:22, 23	11:34–36	134
36	Woe 1: Dishes	23:25, 26	11:39b–41	135
	Woe 2: Tithing	23:23	11:42	135
	Woe 3: Status Seeking	23:6, 7	11:43	135
	Woe 4: Unknown Graves	23:27, 28	11:44	135
	Woe 5: Burdens	23:4	11:46	135
	Woe 6: Tombs of the Prophets	23:29–31	11:47, 48	135
	Wisdom Saying: Murder of the Prophets	23:34–36	11:49–51	135
	Woe 7: Key of Knowledge	23:13	11:52	135
	G. On Acknowledgement			
37	Hidden and Revealed	10:26	12:2	136
	Secret and Open	10:27	12:3	136
38	No Fear of People	10:28	12:4, 5	136
	More Value Than Sparrows	10:29–31	12:6, 7	136

No.		Matt.	Luke	Page
39	Acknowledgement of Jesus	10:32, 33	12:8, 9	136
40	Blaspheming Against the Spirit	12:32	12:10	136
41	Assistance of the Spirit in Court	10:19	12:11, 12	137
42	[Flight through the Towns of Israel]	10:23	—	137

H. On Proper Concerns

No.		Matt.	Luke	Page
43	Against Cares and Concerns	6:25–33	12:22–31	137
	(Little Flock)	—	12:32	138
44	Treasure in Heaven	6:19–21	12:33, 34	138
45	Readiness	—	12:35	138
	The Watchful Servants	—	12:36–38	138
46	The Householder and the Thief	24:43, 44	12:39, 40	139
47	The Faithful and Unworthy Servant	24:45–51	12:42–46	139
48	Fire on the Earth/Baptism	—	12:49, 50	139
	Dissensions	10:34–36	12:51–53	139

I. Parables

No.		Matt.	Luke	Page
49	(Signs of the Time)	16:2, 3	12:54-56	140
50	Settlement with an Accuser	5:25, 26	12:57–59	140
51	Jerusalem Saying	23:37–39	13:34, 35	140
52	Mustard Seed	13:31, 32	13:18, 19	140
	Leaven	13:33	13:20, 21	141
53	Narrow Gate	7:13, 14	13:23, 24	141
54	The Shut Door	7:22, 23	13:25–27	141
55	From East and West	8:11, 12	13:28, 29	141
56	The Last and the First	20:16	13:30	141
57	(The Great Banquet)	22:1–10	14:15–24	141
58	Discipleship—"Taking the Cross"	10:37, 38	14:25–27	142
59	Tasteless Salt	5:13	14:34, 35	142

No.		Matt.	Luke	Page
60	[The Sheep in the Pit]	12:11, 12	14:5	142
61	The Lost Sheep	18:12–14	15:3–7	142
	(The Lost Drachma)	—	15:8–10	143
62	Violence Saying	11:12, 13	16:16	143
63	Continuance of the Law	5:18	16:17	143
64	Divorce	5:32	16:18	143
65	Serving Two Masters	6:24	16:13	143

J. On the Responsibility of Disciples

No.		Matt.	Luke	Page
66	Offenses	18:7	17:1, 2	144
67	Forgiveness	18:21, 22	17:3, 4	144
68	Faith	17:20	17:5, 6	144

K. On Judgment

No.		Matt.	Luke	Page
69	Against False Messianic Expectation	24:26	17:22, 23	144
	Interpretive Saying: Like the Lightning	24:27	17;24	144
	The Corpse and Vultures	24:28	17:37	144
70	As in Noah's Time	24:37–39a	17:26, 27	145
	As in Lot's Time	24:39b	17:28–30	145
71	Resoluteness and Flight	24:17, 18	17:31, 32	145
72	Finding Life	10:39	17:33	145
73	Two End Time Fates	24:40, 41	17:34, 35	145
74	[Participation in Judgment]	19:28	22:28–30	145
75	[Talents]	25:14–30	19:12–27	146

Appendix I. Texts Possibly Pertaining to Q

No.		Matt.	Luke	Page
4a	Arrival of Jesus	4:12, 13	4:14–16	147
5a	Woe Sayings	—	6:24–26	147
26a	The Friend at Midnight	—	11:5–8	147
36a	The Leaven of the Pharisees	—	12:1b	148

No.		Matt.	Luke	Page
47a	Care and Responsibility	—	12:47, 48	148
56a	Exaltation and Humiliation	23:12	14:11	148
63a	Validity of the Commandments	5:19	—	148
68a	A Servant's Duty	—	17:7–10	148

Sayings of the Lord Jesus

Mt   Lk

A. Introduction

1

3:1-2   1   In *those days* **John** *came,*   3:2b,3b
         2 **preaching in the wilderness** <*a baptism* **of repentance**>;

3:3   3 *as* **it is written** *by* **the prophet Isaiah,**   3:4
         4 **"A voice of one crying in the wilderness,**
         5 **'Prepare the way of the Lord,**
         6 **make his paths straight.'"**

3:5b   7 **And** *he went into* **all the region about the Jordan.**   3:3a

         2

3:7   1   *And* **he said** *to the multitudes* **coming** *for* **his baptism,** 3:7
         2 **"You brood of vipers!**
         3 **Who warned you to flee from the wrath to come?**

3:8   4 **Bear fruit therefore that befits repentance,**
3:9   5   **and** *do* **not** *begin* **to say to yourselves,**
         6   **'We have Abraham as our father';**
         7 **for I tell you that God is able**
         8   **from these stones to raise up children to Abraham.**

3:10   9 **Even now the axe is laid to the root of the trees;**   3:9
         10   **every tree therefore that does not bear good fruit is cut down**
         11   **and thrown into the fire.**

3:11   12 **I baptize you** *with* **water,**   3:16
         13 **but he who is mightier than I is coming** *after me;*
         14   **I am not worthy**
         15   *to untie the thong* **of his sandals;**
         16   **he will baptize you with the holy Spirit and with fire.**

Mt			Lk
3:12	17	**His winnowing fork is in his hand,**	3:17
	18	**and he will clear his thresing floor**	
	19	**and gather his wheat into the granary,**	
	20	**but the chaff he will burn with unquenchable fire."**	

3

3:13	1	[*And Jesus came to John*	3:21
	2	**to be baptized** *by him,*	
3:16	3	**and when Jesus had been baptized, the heaven was opened**	
	4	**and the Spirit descended upon him** <**as a dove**>,	3:22
3:17	5	**and a voice from heaven** *came,*	
	6	*"You are* **my Son;**	
	7	*today I have begotten you.'*]	

4

4:1	1	*And* **Jesus was led up** *by* **the Spirit** *in* **the wilderness**	4:1
	2	**to be tempted by the devil,**	4:2
4:2	3	**and he ate nothing for forty days,**	
	4	*and* **afterward he was hungry.**	
4:3	5	*And* **the devil said to him,**	4:3
	6	**"If you are the Son of God,**	
	7	**command this stone to become bread."**	
4:4	8	*And Jesus* **answered,**	4:4
	9	**"It is written,**	
	10	**'You shall not live by bread alone.'"**	
4:5	11	*And the devil* **took him to Jerusalem**	4:9
	12	**and set** *him* **on the pinnacle of the temple,**	
4:6	13	**and said to him,**	
	14	**"If you are the Son of God,**	
	15	**throw yourself down;**	
	16	**for it is written,**	4:10
	17	**'He will give his angels charge of you,'**	
	18	**and 'on their hands they will bear you up**	4:11
	19	**lest you strike your foot against a stone.'"**	
4:7	20	*And* **Jesus answered him,**	4:12
	21	*"Again* **it is written,**	
	22	**'You shall not tempt the Lord your God.'"**	
4:8	23	*And* **the devil took him** *to a very high mountain*	4:5
	24	**and showed him all the kingdoms of the world**	
	25	**and the glory of them,**	
4:9	26	**and he said to him,**	4:6
	27	**"All these I will give you,** | **if you will worship me."**	

Mt			Lk
4:10	28	*And* **Jesus answered him,**	4:8
	29	**"It is written,**	
	30	**'You shall worship the Lord your God,**	
	31	**and him only shall you serve.'"**	
4:11	32	*Then* **the devil left him.**	4:13

B. Sermon on the Mount

4:12–13			*4a (App I pg 147)* 4:14–15
		5	
5:1-2	1	*(And Jesus went up)* **on the mountain,**	6:12a,17
	2	**and seeing** *the* **crowds and his disciples,**	
	3	**he said,**	
5:3	4	**"Blessed are the poor,**	6:20b
	5	**for** *theirs* **is the kingdom of God.**	
5:6	6	**Blessed are those who hunger** *now,*	6:21
	7	**for they shall be satisfied.**	
5:4	8	**Blessed are those who weep now,**	
	9	**for they shall be comforted.**	
5:11	10	**Blessed are you when** *(people) hate you*	6:22
	11	*and* **exclude and revile you**	
	12	**and** *utter* **evil** *against* **you**	
	13	**on account of** *the son of man.*	
5:12	14	**Rejoice and be glad,**	6:23
	15	*for* **your reward is great in heaven:**	
	16	**for so** *their ancestors* **did to the prophets."**	
—			*5a (App I pg 147)* 6:24-26
		6	
5:44	1	**I say to you,**	6:27
	2	**love your enemies;**	
	3	*do good to those who hate you;*	
	4	*bless those who curse you;*	6:28
	5	**pray for those who abuse you.**	
5:39b	6	**To whoever strikes you on the right cheek,**	6:29
	7	**turn the other as well.**	
5:40	8	**And let** *whoever would sue you and* **take your coat**	
	9	**have your cloak as well.**	
5:41	10	*(And to whoever forces you to go one mile,*	—
	11	*go two miles with that one.)*	
5:42	12	**Give to whoever begs from you,**	6:30
	13	**and do not refuse** *whoever would* **borrow from you.**	
5:46	14	**For if you love those who love you,**	6:32

Mt   Lk
     15   **what reward have you?**
     16   **Do not even sinners do the same?**
5:47 17 **And if you salute your own,**   6:33
     18   **what** *reward have you?*
     19   **Do not even the Gentiles do the same?**

—   20 [*I say to you,*]   6:35
     21 *love your enemies,*
5:45 22 **and you will be sons of God,**
     23 **for he makes his sun rise on the good and evil.**

                          7
5:48 1   *You* **must be merciful,**   6:36
     2   **even as your Father is merciful.**

7:1 3   *And* **judge not,** *and* **you will not be judged:**   6:37
7:2a 4   *and condemn not and* **you will** *not* **be condemned:**
     5   *forgive, and you will be forgiven.*

—   6   *Give, and it will be given to you;*   6:38
     7   *good measure, pressed down,*
     8   *shaken together, running over,*
     9   *will be put into your lap.*
7:2b 10 **For the measure you give, will be the measure you receive.**

                          8
7:12 1   *So what* **you wish, that others would do to you,**   6:31
     2   **do** *so* **to them as well.**

                          9
15:14 1 *Can* **one who is blind lead another who is blind?**   6:39
     2   **Will they** *not* **both fall into a pit?**

10:24 3 **The disciple is not above the teacher:**   6:40
10:25a 4 [*it is enough for the disciple*
     5   *to* **be]** **like the teacher.**

                          10
7:3 1   **And why do you see the speck that is in your friend's eye,** 6:41
     2   **but do not notice the log** *that* **is in your own eye?**
7:4 3   *Or* **how can you say to your friend, "Let me take that speck**
                                              out of your eye," 6:42
     4   *when there is* **the log in your own eye?**
7:5 5   **You hypocrite, first take the log out of your own eye,**
     6   **and then you will see clearly to take the speck** *out of* **your**
                                                        friend's eye.

Mt   Lk

11

7:18   1 *For* no good tree bears bad fruit;   6:43
        2   nor again does a bad tree bear good fruit,
12:33c 3 for *each* tree is known by its fruit.   6:44
7:16b   4 Are figs gathered from thorns
        5   or grapes from a bramble bush?

12:35   6 One who is good brings forth good things out of the good   6:45
                                                                      treasure
        7   and one who is evil brings forth evil things out of that which
                                                                      is evil,
12:34b 8 for the mouth speaks out of the abundance of the heart.

12

7:21   1 *And why do* you call me, "Lord, Lord!"   6:46
        2   and do *not* do *what I tell you?*

7:24   3 <*I will show you*> what each one   6:47
        4   who hears my words and does them *is like.*
        5 Such a one is like someone who built a house upon the rock,   6:48
7:25   6 *and the rain fell* and the floods came
        7   *and the winds blew and beat* upon that house,
        8 but it did not fall,
        9   because it had been founded on the rock.
7:26   10 *And everyone* who hears *my words* and does not do them,   6:49
       11 is like someone who built a house upon the sand,
7:27   12 *and the rain fell and* the floods came,
       13   *and the winds blew and beat upon that house,*
       14 and it fell
       15   and great was the fall of it.

13

7:28a   1   *And* when Jesus finished   7:1
        2   *these* sayings,
8:5a   3   he entered Capernaum.

8:5b,6 4   And a centurion [came forward to him | beseeching,   7:2-6a
        5   "*Lord,* my servant *is lying at home*
        6   *paralyzed, in terrible distress.*"
8:7   7   *And he said to him,* "I will come and heal him."
8:8   8   *And the* centurion *answered him and* said,]   7:6b
        9 "Lord, I am not worthy
       10 to have you come under my roof;
       11 but say the word, and my servant will be healed.   7:7

Mt   Lk
8:9   12 For I am a man under authority   7:8
         13 with soldiers under me,
         14 and I say to one, 'Go,' and he goes,
         15 and to another, 'Come,' and he comes,
         16 and to my slave, 'Do this,' and he does it."   ‹
8:10   17   When Jesus heard him, he marveled   7:9
         18   and said to those who followed him,
         19 "[*Truly*], I say to you,
         20 not even in Israel have I found such faith."
8:13   21   [And *his* servant was healed *at that very moment*.]   7:10

         C. John the Baptist
              14
11:2   1   *Now when* John   7:18
         2   *heard <in prison>* of all these things,
         3   he sent *two* of his disciples [*to the Lord*]   7:19
11:3   4   saying, "Are you the one who is to come or shall we look
                                                for another?"
11:4   5   And Jesus answered them,   7:22
         6 "Go and tell John what you see and hear:
11:5   7   the blind receive their sight *and* the lame walk,
         8   lepers are cleansed and the deaf hear,
         9   the dead are raised up, *and* the poor have good news preached
                                                to them,
11:6   10 and whoever takes no offense at me is blessed."   7:23

              15
11:7   1   As *these* went away, [*Jesus*] began to speak   7:24
         2   to the crowds concerning John,
         3 "What did you go out into the wilderness to behold?
         4   A reed shaken by the wind?
11:8   5 What then did you go out to see?   7:25
         6   A man clothed in soft raiment?
         7   Behold, those *who wear soft raiment* are in kings' *houses.*
11:9   8 What then did you go out to see?   7:26
         9   A prophet?
         10 Yes, I tell you,
         11   and more than a prophet.

11:10   12 This is he of whom it is written,   7:27
         13   'Behold, I send my messenger before your face,
         14   who shall prepare your way before you.'

11:11   15 I tell you,   7:28

Mt   Lk

16 **among those born of women** *there has risen* **no one greater
than John;**

17 **yet whoever is least in the kingdom of God is greater than he."**

16

11:16	1 **To what then shall I compare this generation**	7:31
	2 *and what is it like?*	
	3 **It is like children sitting in the market place**	7:32
11:17	4 **and calling to their playmates — they say,**	
	5 **"We piped to you, and you did not dance;**	
	6 **we wailed, and you did not mourn."**	
11:18	7 **For John came neither eating nor drinking,**	7:33
	8 **and you say, "He has a demon."**	
11:19	9 **The son of man came eating and drinking,**	7:34
	10 **and you say, "Behold, a glutton and a drunkard,**	
	11 **a friend of tax collectors and sinners."**	
	12 **Yet wisdom is justified by her** *children.*	7:35

D. Mission of the Disciples

17

8:19	1 **And** <*along the road*> **someone said to him,**	9:57
	2 **"I will follow you wherever you go."**	
8:20	3 **And Jesus said to that person,**	9:58
	4 **"Foxes have holes,**	
	5 **and birds of the air have nests;**	
	6 **but the son of man has no-**	
	7 **where to lay his head."**	
8:21	8 **But another said** *to him,*	9:59
	9 **"Lord, let me first**	
	10 **go** *and* **bury my father."**	
8:22	11 **But** *Jesus* **said to that person,**	9:60
	12 **"Follow** *me,*	
	13 **and leave the dead to bury their own dead."**	
—	14 *But another said,*	9:61
	15 *"I will follow you, Lord;*	
	16 *but let me first*	
	17 *say farewell to those at my home."*	
	18 *But Jesus said to that person,*	9:62
	19 *"No one who puts a hand to the plow*	
	20 *and looks back*	
	21 *is fit for the kingdom of God."*	

Mt   Lk

18

—   1   *<And the Lord appointed seventy-two*   10:1
            2   *and* **sent** *them two by two* **into every town.>**
9:37a   3   *And* **he said to them,**   10:2a

9:37b   4   **"The harvest is plentiful, but the laborers are few;**   10:2
9:38   5   **pray therefore the Lord of the harvest**
            6   **to send out laborers into his harvest."**

19

10:16a   1   *Go your way;* **behold, I send you out**   10:3
            2   **as lambs in the midst of wolves.**

20

10:5b   1   *(Go nowhere among the Gentiles,*   —
            2   *and enter no town of the Samaritans,*
10:6   3   *but go rather to the lost sheep of the house of Israel.)*

21

10:9,10a   1   *Carry* **no** *purse,* **no bag, no sandals;**   10:4
            2   **and** *salute no one on the* **road.**

10:11a   3   **Whatever house you enter,**   10:5
10:12   4   *first say, "Peace be to this house!"*
10:13   5   **And if** *a child of peace* **is** *there,*   10:6
            6   **let your peace come upon that one,**
            7   **but if not,** *let your peace* **return** *to* **you.**

10:11b   8   *And* **remain** *in the same house,*   10:7
            9   *eating and drinking what they provide;*
10:10b   10   **for the laborer deserves a wage;**
           11   *do not go from house to house.*

10:11a   12   *And* **whenever you enter a town**   10:8
—   13   *and they receive you,*
10:8a   14   **heal** *the* **sick**   10:9
10:7   15   *and* **say** *to them,*
           16   **"The kingdom of God has come near** *to you."*
10:14   17   *But* **whenever** *you enter a town*   10:10
           18   **and they do not receive you,**
           19   **as you leave** *that* **town**
           20   **shake off the dust from your feet.**   10:11

Mt   Lk
10:15   21 I tell you,   10:12
        22 *that* it shall be more tolerable on *that* day for Sodom than for that
                                                                        town.

                        22
11:21   1 Woe to you, Chorazin!   10:13
         2   Woe to you, Bethsaida!
         3 For if in Tyre and Sidon
         4   had been done the works done in you,
         5   they would have repented long ago in sackcloth and ashes.
11:22   6 But *I tell you,*   10:14
         7 it shall be more tolerable in the judgment for Tyre and Sidon than
                                                                    for you.

11:23   8 And you, Capernaum, will you be exalted to heaven?   10:15
         9   You shall be brought down to Hades.

                        23
10:40   1 *Whoever hears* you *hears* me,   10:16
         2 *and whoever rejects you rejects me;*
         3 and whoever *rejects* me *rejects* him who sent me.

                        24
11:25   1   <At that hour *Jesus rejoiced in the Spirit*>   10:21
         2   *and* said,

         3 "I thank you, Father,
         4   Lord of heaven and earth,
         5 that you have hidden these things from the wise and understanding
         6   and revealed them to babes.
11:26   7 Yes, Father,
         8 for so it was well-pleasing to you.

11:27   9 All things have been delivered to me by my Father;   10:22
        10 and no one knows the Son except the Father,
        11 no one the Father except the Son
        12   and anyone to whom the Son chooses to reveal him."

                        25
13:16   1 Blessed are the eyes which see *what you see!*   10:23b
13:17   2 *For* I tell you   10:24

Mt   Lk

    3 **that many prophets and** *kings*
    4   **longed to see what you see, and did not see it**
    5   **and to hear what you hear, and did not hear it.**

E. On Prayer

    26

6:9   1 *When* **you pray,** *say:*   11:2

    3 **"Father,**
    3 **hallowed be thy name.**
6:10   4   **Thy kingdom come.**
6:11   5 **Give us this day our daily bread.**   11:3
6:12   6 **And forgive us our debts,**   11:4
    7   **as we also have forgiven our debtors;**
6:13   8 **and lead us not into temptation."**
—   *26a (App I pg 147)* 11:5-8

    27

    1 *I tell you,*   11:9
7:7   2 **ask, and it will be given you;**
    3   **seek, and you will find;**
    4   **knock, and it will be opened to you.**
7:8   5 **For everyone who asks receives,**   11:10
    6   **and whoever seeks finds**
    7   **and to the one who knocks it will be opened.**

    28

7:9   1 **Which of you,**   11:11a
    2 *if your* **child asks for a loaf,**   11:12
    3   **will give a stone?**
7:10   4 **Or if the child asks for a fish,**   11:11b
    5   **will give a serpent?**
7:11   6 **If you then, who are evil,**   11:13
    7   **know how to give good gifts to your children,**
    8 **how much more will the heavenly Father**
    9   **give** *good things* **to those who ask him.**

F. Controversies

    29

12:22   1   *And he was casting out* **a demon,**   11:14

Mt			Lk
	2	*and it was* **dumb.**	
	3	**And when the demon had gone out, the person who was dumb spoke,**	
12:23	4	**and the people marveled.**	
12:24	5	*But some of them* **said,**	11:15
	6	**"By Beelzebul, the prince of demons,**	
	7	**he casts out demons."**	
12:25	8	**But knowing their thoughts, he said to them,**	11:17

	9	**"Every kingdom divided against itself is laid waste,**	
	10	**and every house** *divided* **against** *itself* **will not stand.**	
12:26	11	**And if Satan is divided against himself,**	11:18
	12	**how will his kingdom stand?**	

12:27	13	**And if I cast out demons by Beezebul**	11:19
	14	**by whom do your children cast them out?**	
	15	**Therefore they shall be your judges.**	
12:28	16	**But if it is by** *the finger* **of God that I cast out demons,**	11:20
	17	**then the kingdom of God has come upon you."**	

30

(12:29)	1	*When* **a strong man** *guards his own* **palace,**	11:21
	2	*his goods are in peace,*	
	3	*but when* **<one>** *stronger* [*than he*] **enters, he will overcome him;**	11:22
	4	**he takes away his armor**	
	5	[**and** *divides* **his** *spoil.*]	

31

12:30	1	**Whoever is not with me is against me,**	11:23
	2	**and whoever does not gather with me scatters.**	

32

12:43	1	**When the unclean spirit has gone out of someone,**	11:24
	2	**it passes through waterless places seeking rest**	
12:44	3	**but finds none;**	**then it says,**	
	4	**"I will return to my house from which I came."**	
	5	**And when it comes, it finds the house swept and put in order.**	11:25
12:45	6	**Then it goes and brings** *with itself*	11:26
	7	**seven other spirits more evil than itself,**	
	8	**and they enter and dwell there;**	
	9	**and the last state of that person is worse than the first.**	

Mt			Lk
		33	
12:38	1	*Some* **said,**	11:16
	2	**"We wish** *to see* **a sign from you."**	
12:39	3	**But** *he began* **to say,**	11:29
	4	*"This generation is* **an evil generation;**	
	5	**it seeks a sign, but no sign shall be given to it**	
	6	**except the sign of Jonah.**	
12:40	7	**For as Jonah became** *a sign to the people of Nineveh,*	11:30
	8	**so will the son of man be** *to this generation."*	

Mt			Lk
		34	
12:42	1	**The queen of the south**	11:31
	2	**will arise at the judgment with this generation**	
	3	**and condemn it;**	
	4	**for she came from the ends of the earth**	
	5	**to hear the wisdom of Solomon**	
	6	**and behold, something greater than Solomon is here.**	
12:41	7	**The people of Nineveh**	11:32
	8	**will arise at the judgment with this generation**	
	9	**and condemn it;**	
	10	**for they repented at the preaching of Jonah,**	
	11	**and behold, something greater than Jonah is here.**	

Mt			Lk
		35	
5:15	1	**People do not** *light* **a lamp**	11:33
	2	**and put** *it* **under a bushel**	
	3	**but on a stand,**	
	4	*and* **it gives light** *to all in the house.*	
6:22	5	*Your* **eye is the lamp of your body;**	11:34
	6	**when your eye is sound,**	
	7	**your whole body is full of light;**	
6:23	8	**but when** *your eye* **is not sound,**	
	9	**your** *whole* **body is full of darkness.**	
	10	*If* **then the light in you is darkness,**	11:35
	11	*how great is the darkness!*	
—	12	*If your whole body is full of light,*	11:36
	13	*it will be wholly bright,*	
	14	*as when a lamp with its rays gives you light.*	

Mt			Lk
	36		
23:25	1	**Woe to you, Pharisees!**	11:39b
	2	**For you cleanse the outside of the cup and of the plate,**	
	3	**but** *the* **inside is full of extortion and rapacity.**	
23:26	4	**You fools!** *Did not he who made the outside*	11:40
	5	*make the inside also?*	
	6	*Cleanse* **the inside,**	11:41
	7	**and** *the outside becomes* **clean.**	
23:23	8	**Woe to you, Pharisees!**	11:42
	9	**For you tithe mint and dill** *and cummin,*	
	10	**and have neglected justice and the love** *of God;*	
	11	**these you ought to have done, without neglecting the others.**	
	12	*Woe to you, Pharisees!*	11:43
23:6	13	*for* **you love the best seat in the synagogues**	
23:7a	14	**and salutations in the market places.**	
23:27	15	**Woe to you,** *Pharisees!*	11:44
	16	**For you are like graves** *which are not seen,*	
	17	*and* **people** *walk over them withou knowing it.*	
	18	*Woe to you,* **lawyers,** *also!*	11:46
23:4	19	*for* **you bind heavy and hard to bear burdens**	
	20	*and* **you lay them** *on* **people's** *shoulders,*	
	21	*but* **you yourselves will not move** *them* **with your finger.**	
23:29	22	**Woe to you!**	11:47
	23	**For you build the tombs of the prophets**	
23:30	24	*and* **your ancestors** *killed them.*	
23:31	25	**So you witness against** *yourselves,*	11:48
	26	[*that* *you are children* **of those who killed** *the prophets*].	
23:34	27	**Therefore** *also the wisdom of God said,*	11:49
	28	**"I will send** *them* **prophets and** *apostles,*	
	29	**some of whom they will kill and persecute,**	
23:35	30	**that** *the* **blood of all** *the prophets*	11:50
	31	*which* **was shed** *from the foundation of the world*	
		may be required (of this generation).	
	32	**From the blood of Abel to the blood of Zechariah**	11:51
	33	*who* **perished between the altar and the sanctuary.**	
23:36	34	*Yes,* **I tell you,**	
	35	*it shall be required of* **this generation."**	
23:13	36	**Woe to you, lawyers!**	11:52

Mt   Lk

37 **For** *you have taken away the* **key** *of knowledge;*
38 *you* **neither enter yourselves,**
39   **nor allow those who would enter** *to go in.*

G. On Acknowledgement

—   *36a (App I pg 148)* 12:1b
                        37
10:26   1 **Nothing is covered**   12:2
        2   **that will not be revealed,**
        3 **hidden**
        4   **that will not be known.**

10:27   5 **What you have said in the dark**   12:3
        6   **shall be heard in the light,**
        7 **and what you have whispered into the ear**
        8   **shall be proclaimed upon the housetops.**

                        38
10:28   1 *But I tell you,*   12:4
        2 **do not fear those who kill the body**
        3   *and after that* **have no** *more that they can do.*
        4   *But I will warn you whom to fear:*
        5 **fear** *the one who, after having killed, has power* 12:5
        6   *to cast into* **hell.**
        7 *Yes, I tell you, fear that one!*

10:29   8 **Are not** *five* **sparrows sold for two pennies?**   12:6
        9 **And not one of them** *will fall to the ground without* **God's will.**
10:30 10 **But even the hairs of your head are all numbered.** 12:7
10:31 11   **Fear not;**
       12   *you* **are of more value than many sparrows.**

  Mt   **39**   Lk
        1 *But I tell you,*   12:8
10:32   2 **every one who acknowledges me before others,**
        3   *the son of man* **also will acknowledge before** *the angels* **of God;**

10:33   4 **but who**ever **denies me before others**   12:9
        5   **will be denied before the angels of God.**

                        40
12:32   1 **And who**ever **says a word against the son of man,**   12:10

Mt   Lk

2   will be forgiven;
3   but who*ever* blasphemes against the holy Spirit,
4   will not be forgiven.

41

10:19   1 And when they bring you *before the synagogues* <*and the* 12:11
                                                          councils>,
        2   do not be anxious how or what you are to say;
        3 for the holy Spirit will teach you in that very hour   12:12
        4   what you are to say.

42

10:23   1 [*When they persecute you in one town,*   —
        2   *flee to the next;*
        3 *truly, I say to you,*
        4 *you will not have gone through all the towns of Israel*
        5   *before the son of man comes.*]

H. On Proper Concerns

43

6:25   1 Therefore I tell you,   12:22
        2 do not be anxious about *your* life, what you shall eat,
        3   nor about *your* body, what you shall put on.
        4 Is *not* life more than food,   12:23
        5   and the body more than clothing?

6:26   6 Look at the ravens,   12:24
        7   they neither sow nor reap
        8   nor *gather into* barns,
        9 and yet God feeds them.
        10 *Of how much* more value are you *than the birds!*

6:27   11 And which of you by being anxious   12:25
        12   can add a cubit to your span of life?
6:28   13 *And* why are you anxious about *clothing?*   12:26

        14 Consider the lilies, how *they grow;*   12:27
        15   they neither *toil* nor spin.
6:29   16 Yet I tell you,
        17 *that* not even Solomon in all his glory
        18   was arrayed like one of these.
6:30   19 But if the grass which is alive in the field today,   12:28

Mt   Lk

20   **and tomorrow is thrown into the oven,**

21   **is so clothed by God,**

22 *how much* **more will he clothe you, who are of little faith?**

6:31   23 *And* **do not be anxious** *saying,*   12:29

24   **"What shall we eat?"** *or* **"What shall we drink?"** *or* **"What shall we wear?"**

6:32   25   **For the Gentiles seek all these things;**   12:30

26 **and your Father knows that you need them.**

6:33   27 *But* **seek** *first* **his kingdom,**   12:31

28   **and these things shall be yours as well.**

—   29 *(Fear not, little flock,*   12:32

30   *for it is your Father's good pleasure*

31   *to give you the kingdom.)*

44

6:19   1 *Do* **not** *make for yourselves* **treasures** *on earth,*   12:33

2   *where moth and rust consume*

3   *and where thieves break in and steal,*

6:20   4 **but make for yourselves treasures in heaven,**

5   *where neither* **moth** *nor* **rust consume**

6   *and* **where thieves do not break in and** *steal.*

6:21   7 **For where your treasure is,**   12:34

8   **there will your heart be also.**

45

—   1 *Let your loins be girded*   12:35

2   *and your lamps burning,*

3 *and be like those who are waiting for their master*   12:36

4   *to come home from the marriage feast,*

5   *so that they may open to him at once when he comes and knocks.*

6 *(Blessed are those servants*   12:37

7   *whom the master finds awake when he comes;*

8 *truly, I say to you,*

9 *he will gird himself and have them sit at table,*

10   *and he will come and serve them.)*

11 <*If he comes in the second watch, or in the third,*   12:38

12   *and finds them so,*

13   *blessed are those servants!*>

Mt		Lk

46

24:43	1 **But know this,**	12:39
	2 **that if the householder had known**	
	3 **at what hour the thief was coming,**	
	4 **he would not have left his house to be broken into.**	
24:44	5 *Therefore,* **you also must be ready,**	12:40
	6 **for the son of man is coming at an hour you do not expect.**	

47

24:45	1 **Who then is the faithful and wise servant,**	12:42
	2 **whom the master has set over his household,**	
	3 **to give** *them* **their food at the proper time?**	
24:46	4 **Blessed is that servant**	12:43
	5 **whom the master, when he comes, will find doing so.**	
24:47	6 *Truly,* **I say to you,**	12:44
	7 **he will set that servant over all his possessions.**	
24:48	8 **But if that servant thinks,**	12:45
	9 **"My master is delayed in coming,"**	
24:49	10 **and begins to beat the other servants,**	
	11 **and eats and drinks** *with the* **drunken,**	
24:50	12 **the master of that servant will come**	12:46
	13 **on a day when he is not expected and at an hour that is not known,**	
24:51	14 **and will punish that one**	
	15 **and place that one among the unfaithful.**	
—	*47a (App I pg 148)*	12:47,48

48

—	1 *I came to cast fire upon the earth;*	12:49
	2 *and would that it were already kindled!*	
	3 *I have a baptism to be baptized with;*	12:50
	4 *and how I am constrained until it is accomplished!*	
10:34	5 **Do you think that I have come to bring peace** *on* **earth?**	12:51
	6 *I tell you,* **not** *peace* **but a sword.**	
(10:36)	7 **For** *in one house five will* **be divided,**	12:52
10:35	8 *three against two and two against three|they will be divided,*	12:53
	9 *father against son and son against* **father,**	
	10 *mother against daughter and* **daughter** *against* **mother,**	

Mt   Lk

11   *mother-in-law against* **her** *daughter-in-law and* **daughter-in-law** *against* **mother-in-law.**

I. Parables

49

16:2   1 [*When you see the cloud rising in the west,*   12:54
        2   **you say,** *"A shower is coming;"*
16:3   3 **and** *when you see the south wind blowing,*   12:55
        4   **you say, "There will be scorching heat."]**
        5 *You hypocrites!* **You know how to interpret the appearance** 12:56
                                                    of the sky,
        6   **but** *why can you* **not** *interpret* **the** *present* **time?**

50

5:25   1 *Make friends quickly* **with your accuser,**   12:58
        2   *while you are going* **with** *that one* **on the way** *to court,*
        3 **lest** *your accuser* **hand you over to the judge**
        4   **and the judge to the guard,**
        5   **and you be put in prison.**
5:26   6 **I say to you, you will never get out**   12:59
        7   **till you have paid the last penny.**

51

23:37   1 **O Jerusalem, Jerusalem,**   13:34
        2   **killing the prophets**
        3   **and stoning those who are sent to you!**
        4 **How often would I have gathered your children together**
        5   **as a hen gathers her brood under her wings**
        6   **and you would not!**

23:38   7 **Behold your house is forsaken.**   13:35
23:39   8 **I tell you, you will not see me until you say,**
        9   **"Blessed is he who comes in the name of the Lord!"**

Mt   **52**   Lk
13:31   1 *What is* **the kingdom of God** *like?*   13:18
        2   *And to what shall I compare it?*
        3 **It is like a grain of mustard seed**   13:19
        4   **which a man took and sowed in his field;**
13:32   5 *and* **it grew and became a tree,**
        6   **and the birds of the air made nests in its branches.**

Mt			Lk
13:33	7	*To what shall I compare* **the kingdom of God?**	13:20
	8	**It is like leaven,**	13:21
	9	**which a woman took and hid in three measures of meal,**	
	10	**till it was all leavened.**	

53

7:13a	1	**Enter by the narrow gate;**	13:24
	2	**for many** *will seek* **to enter**	
7:14b	3	**and** *few* **will find it.**	

54

—	1	*When the householder has risen up and shut the door,*	13:25
	2	*you will begin to stand outside [and to knock at the door],*	
		saying,	
	3	**"Lord,** *Lord,* **open to us."**	
	4	*And he will answer you,*	
	5	*"I do not know where you come from."*	
7:22	6	**Then** *you will begin* **to say,**	13:26
	7	*"We ate and drank in your presence,*	
	8	**and** *you taught in our streets."*	
7:23	9	**And he will say to you,**	13:27
	10	**"I do not know** *where* **you** *come from;*	
	11	**depart from me, you workers of iniquity!"**	

55

8:11	1	*<I tell you*	
	2	*that>* **many will come from east and west and sit at table**	13:29
	3	*with* **Abraham, Isaac, and Jacob**	13:28b
	4	*and all the prophets* **in the kingdom of God,**	
8:12	5	**but** *you* **will be thrown** *into the* **outer** *darkness.*	
	6	**There people will weep and gnash their teeth.**	13:28a

56

20:16	1	**Some** *are* **last who will be first,**	13:30
	2	*and* **some** *are* **first who** *will be* **last.**	
23:12		*56a (App I pg 148)*	14:11

57

22:2	1	**A man gave a** *great* **banquet**	14:16
	2	*and* **invited** *many,*	
22:3,4	3	**and sent his servant** *to say* **to those who had been invited,**	14:17

Mt   Lk

4   *"Come; for all is now* **ready,"**
5   **but** *they would* **not come.**

22:5,6   6 . . .   14:18-20
7   *and the servant reported this to his master.*   14:21a

22:7,8a   8 **Then** *the householder* **in anger said to his servant,**
22:9   9   **"Go out into the thoroughfares,**   14:23b
10   **and** *compel people to come in."*

22:10   11 *And* **the house was filled** *with guests.*
12 *I tell you,*   14:24

22:8b   13   *none* **of those invited** *shall taste my banquet.*

                                    58
10:37   1 *If any one comes to me*   14:26
2   *and does not hate* **father** *and* **mother**
3   *and* **son** *and daughter,*
4 *that one cannot be my* **disciple.**

10:38   5 *And* **whoever does not take up one's cross**   14:27
6   **and come after me,**
7 *cannot be my* **disciple.**

                                    59
1 **Salt** *is good,*   14:34
5:13   2 **but if salt has lost its taste,**
3   **how shall its saltiness be restored?**
4 *It is fit neither* **for** *the land nor for the dunghill;*   14:35
5   *people* **throw** *it* **away.**
6   *<Those who have ears to hear, let them hear.>*

                                    60
12:11   1 [**Who** *among* **you** *who has one* **sheep,**   14:5
2   *if it* **falls into a pit on the sabbath,**
3 *will* **not** *lay hold of* **it** *and* **lift it out?**]

                                    61
18:12   1 **What man** *of you, having* **a hundred sheep,**   15:4
2   **if he has lost one of them,**
3 **does not leave the ninety-nine** *in the wilderness*
4   **and go** *in search of the one which is lost, until* **he finds it?**
18:13   5   *And when he has found it, he lays it on his shoulders, rejoicing.* 15:5
6   *And when he comes home,*   15:6

Mt   Lk

7   *he calls together his friends and his neighbors,*

8   *saying to them, "Rejoice with me,*

9   *for I have found my sheep which was lost."*

10 **I tell you,**   15:7

11 *just so, there will be more* **joy** *in heaven*

12   **over** *one sinner who repents*

13   **than over ninety-nine** *righteous persons*

14   <*who need no repentance*>.

15 *Or what woman, having ten drachmas,*   15:8

—   16 *if she loses one drachma,*

17 *does not light a lamp and sweep the house*

18   *and seek until she finds it?*

19   *And when she has found it, she calls together her friends* 15:9
                                  and neighbors,

20   *saying, "Rejoice with me,*

21   *for I have found the drachma which I had lost."*

22 *I tell you,*   15:10

23 *just so, there is joy before God*

24   *over one sinner who repents.*

62

11:13   1 **The law and the prophets were until John;**   16:16

11:12   2 **since** *then* **the kingdom of God has suffered violence,**

         3   **and** *the violent take* **it** *by force.*

63

5:18   1 *Truly, I say to you,*   16:17

        2 *till* **heaven and earth pass away,**

        3   *not* **a dot** *will pass away from* **the law.**

5:19   *63a (App I pg 148)*   —

64

5:32   1 **Every one who divorces his wife** *(and marries another)* 16:18

        2   **commits adultery,**

        3 **and who**ever **marries a divorced woman**

        4   **commits adultery.**

65

6:24   1 **No one can serve two masters;**   16:13

Mt   Lk

   2   **for either you will hate the one and love the other,**
   3   **or will be devoted to the one and despise the other.**
   4 **You cannot serve God and mammon.**

   J. On the Responsibility of Disciples

                66
18:7   1 **Stumbling blocks** *are sure* **to come,**   17:1
        2 **but woe** *to the one* **by whom** *the stumbling block* **comes.**
18:6   3   **[It would be better for such a one**   17:2
        4   **if a** *great* **millstone were hung around the neck**
        5   **and that person were cast into the sea**
        6   *than that* **one of these little ones should be caused to stumble.]**

                67
18:15,21   **If your friend sins, give a rebuke,**   17:3
        2   *and* **if** *the friend repents, grant forgiveness;*
18:22   3 *and if* **the friend sins against** *you* **seven times** *in the day*   17:4
        4   *and turns seven times, and* **says,** *"I repent,"*
        5   **you must forgive that one.**

                68
17:20   1 **If you have faith as a grain of mustard seed,**   17:6
        2 **you** *could* **say** *to* **this** *sycamine tree,*
        3   *"Be rooted up,* **and** *be planted in the sea,"*
           and *it* **would** *obey* **you.**

—   *68a (App I pg 148)* 17:7-10

   K. On Judgment
                69
24:26   1 *If* **they say to you,**   17:23
        2   **"Lo,** *he is in the wilderness,"*
        3 **do not go out;**
        4   **"Lo,** *he is in the inner rooms,"*
        5 **do not believe it.**

24:27   6 **For as lightening comes** *from the east*   17:24
        7   **and shines** *as far as the west,*
        8 **so will the son of man be** *in his day.*

24:28   9 **Where the** *corpse* **is,**   17:37c
        10   **there the vultures will be gathered together.**

Mt   Lk

70

24:37   1 **As were the days of Noah,**   17:26
        2 **so will it be in the days of the son of man.**
24:38   3 **They ate, they drank, they married, they were given in marriage,** 17:27
        4 **until the day when Noah entered the ark,**
        5 **and** *they did not know until* **the flood came and destroyed**
                                                              them all.

—   6 *And as it was in the days of Lot,*   17:28
        7 *they ate, they drank, they bought, they sold, they planted,*
                                                              they built,
        8 *but on the day when Lot went out from Sodom,*   17:29
        9 *fire and brimstone rained from heaven and destroyed them all.*
24:39b 10 *So* **will** *it* **be** *on the day when* **the son of man** *is revealed.* 17:30

71

(24:17) 1 *On that day, let* **whoever** *is* **on the housetop,**   17:31
        2   **not go down to take what is** *in* **the house;**
(24:18) 3 **and let whoever is in the field not turn back.**   17:32
—   4   [*Remember Lot's wife!*]

72

10:39   1 **Whoever** *finds* **one's life**   17:33
        2   **will lose it,**
        3 *but* **who**ev*er* **loses** *one's life*
        4   *will find* **it.**

73

        1 *I tell you,*   17:34
24:40   2 *in that night* **there will be two men** *in* **one bed;**
        3   **one will be taken and** *one* **left.**
24:41   4 *There will be* **two women grinding** *at the mill;*   17:35
        5   **one will be taken and** *one* **left.**

74

19:28   1 [**You** *who have followed* **me**   22:28
        2   *...* **in the** *kingdom*   22:29,30a
        3   **will sit on twelve thrones,**   22:30b
        4   **judging the twelve tribes of Israel.**]

Mt		75	Lk
25:14	1	[*When* **a man** *was going on a journey,* **he called** *his* **servants**	19:12
	2	**and gave to them** *his property.*	19:13
	3	...	
25:19	4	*Now after a long time the master* **of those servants came**	19:15
	5	**and** *settled accounts with them.*	
25:20	6	**And** *the first* **came, saying,**	19:16
	7	**"Lord, your talent has made** *ten* **talents more."**	
25:21	8	**And** *the master* **said to that one,**	19:17
	9	**"Well done, good servant, you have been faithful over a little,**	
	10	*I will set you* **over** *much."*	
25:22	11	**And** *the second* **came, saying,**	19:18
	12	**"Lord, your talent has made** *five* **talents more."**	
25:23	13	**And the** *master* **said to that one,**	19:19
	14	*"Well done, good servant, you have been faithful over a little,*	
	15	*I will set you* **over** *much."*	
25:24	16	**And** *another* **came, saying,**	19:20
	17	**"Lord,** *I knew* **you to be a hard man;**	
	18	**you reap what you did not sow and you take up what you did not lay down,**	
25:25	19	**and being afraid,** *I hid* **your talent in** *the ground.*	19:21
	20	**Here you have what is yours."**	
25:26	21	*The master* **said to that one, "You wicked servant, you knew**	19:22
	22	**that I reap what I did not sow and I take up what I did not lay down?**	
25:27	23	*Why then did you not invest* **my money** *with the* **bankers?**	19:23
	24	**And at my coming, I should** *have received what was my own* **with interest."**	
25:28	25	*And he said,*	19:24
	26	**"Take the talent from this one,**	
	27	**and give it to the one who has the ten talents."**	
25:29	28	*I tell you,*	19:26
	29	**that to everyone who has, will more be given,**	
	30	**but from the one who has not, even what that one has will be taken away.]**	

TEXTS POSSIBLY PERTAINING TO Q

Mt		**4a**	Lk
4:12b	1	*And Jesus came* **into Galilee**	4:14a
4:23	2	**teaching in their synagogues** *and preaching*	4:15a
	3	*and healing <every disease and every infirmity.>*	
4:13	4	*And leaving* **Nazareth,**	4:16a
	5	*he dwelt in Capernaum by the sea,*	
4:24a	6	**and a report of him went out** *through* **all the** *surrounding*	4:14b
		country.	

		5a	
—	1	*Woe to the rich,*	6:24
	2	*for they have received their consolation;*	
	3	*woe to those who are full now,*	6:25
	3	*for they shall hunger;*	
	5	*woe to those who laugh now,*	
	6	*for they shall mourn;*	
	7	*woe when people speak well of you,*	6:26
	8	*for so their ancestors did to the false prophets.*	

		26a	
—	1	*And he said to them,*	11:5
	2	*"Which of you who has a friend*	
	3	*will go to him at midnight and say to him,*	
	4	*'Friend, lend me three loaves;*	11:6
	5	*<for a friend of mine has arrived on a journey,*	
	6	*and I have nothing to set before him.' >*	
	7	*And he will answer from within,*	11:7

Mt   Lk

  8 *'Do not bother me;*
  9   *<the door is now shut,*
 10   *and my children are with me in bed;*
 11   *I cannot get up and give you anything' >?*
 12 *I tell you,*   11:8
 13 *he will rise and give him whatever he needs."*

36a

—   1 **Beware** *of the leaven of the Pharisees,*   12:1
    2   *which is hypocrisy.*

47a

—   1 *The servant who knew the master's will*   12:47
    2   *but did not act according to his will*
    3   *shall receive a severe beating;*
    4 *but the one who did not know and did what deserved a beating* 12:48
    5   *shall receive a light beating.*

    6 *Of everyone to whom much is given, much will be required,*
    7   *and of one to whom people commit much, they will demand*
                                                    the more.

56a

23:12   1 *Everyone* **who exalts self will be humbled,**   14:11/
        2   **and whoever humbles self will be exalted.**   18:14

63a

5:19   1 *Whoever relaxes one of the least of these commandments*   —
       2   *and so teaches others,*
       3   *shall be called least in the kingdom of God;*
       4 *but whoever does them and teaches them*
       5   *shall be called great in the kingdom of God.*

68a

—   1 *Will any one of you, who has a servant plowing or keeping sheep,* 17:7
    2 *say to him when he has come in from the field, "Sit down at*
                                                    table at once"?
    3   *<Does he thank the servant,*   17:9
    4   *because the servant did what was commanded?>*
    5 *So you also, when you have done all, say,*   17:10
    6 *"We are unworthy servants."*

Appendix II.
INTRODUCTORY PHRASES POSSIBLY
PERTAINING TO Q

Lk	1	Q no.
10:23a	And turning to the disciples, he said privately,	25
	2	
11:1	And one of his disciples said,	26
	"Lord, teach us to pray,	
	as also John taught his disciples."	
11:2a	And he said to them,	
	3	
11:37	A Pharisee asked him to dine with him	36
11:38	and was astonished to see that he did not wash before dinner.	
11:39a	And the Lord said to him,	
	4	
11:45	One of the lawyers answered him,	36, 18
	"Teacher, in saying this you reproach us also."	
	And he said,	
	5	
12:1a	He began to say to his disciples,	37
	6	
12:22a	And he said to his disciples,	43
	7	
12:41	And one of the disciples said,	47

Lk		Q no.
	"Lord, are you telling these for us or for all?"	
12:42a	And the Lord said,	
	8	
12:54a	And he said to the multitudes,	49
	9	
13:18a	He said therefore,	52
	10	
13:20a	And again he said,	52, 7
	11	
13:23	And someone said to him,	53
	"Lord, will those who are saved be few?"	
	And he said to them,	
	12	
14:5a	And Jesus said to the lawyers,	60
	13	
14:15	Someone said to him,	57
	"Blessed is the one who shall eat bread in the kingdom of God!"	
14:16a	And Jesus spoke to them,	
	14	
14:25	And turning, he said to the multitudes,	58
	15	
17:1a	And he said to his disciples,	66
	16	
17:5	And the disciples said to the Lord,	68
	"Increase our faith!"	
17:6a	And the Lord said,	
	17	
17:22a	And he said to the disciples,	69
	18	
17:37a	And they said to him,	69,9
	"Where, Lord?"	
	He said to them,	

Lk		Q no.
	19	
19:11	And Jesus proceeded to say,	75
	20	
Mt 19:28a	Jesus said to the disciples,	74
	21	
Lk 11:5a	And he said to them,	26a

Appendix III.
MARCAN PASSAGES PARALLEL TO Q

		Q
Mk	*1*	*no. 1*
1:2	As it is written in Isaiah the prophet,	*3*
	"Behold, I send my messenger before your face,	*(15:13)*
	who shall prepare your way;	*(15:14)*
1:3	a voice of one crying in the wilderness:	*4*
	'Prepare the way of the Lord;	*5*
	make his paths straight'—"	*6*
1:4	John the baptizer appeared in the wilderness,	*1*
	[and] preaching a baptism of repentance for the forgiveness of sins.	*2*
1:5	And there went out to him all the country of Judea,	(2:1)
	and all the people of Jerusalem;	
	and they were baptized by him in the river Jordan,	
	confessing their sins.	
	2	no. 2
1:7	And he preached, saying,	1
	"After me comes he who is mightier than I;	13
	I am not worthy	14
	to stoop down and untie the thong of his sandals.	15
1:8	I have baptized you with water,	12
	but he will baptize you with the holy Spirit."	16
	3	no. 3
1:9	And it happened in those days,	1

153

Mk		Q
	that Jesus came from Nazareth of Galilee	
	and was baptized by John in the Jordan.	2
1:10	And immediately coming up out of the water,	3
	he saw the heavens opened	
	and the Spirit descending upon him like a dove.	4
1:11	And a voice [came] from heaven,	5
	"You are my beloved Son;	6
	with you I am well pleased."	7

4   no.4

1:12	And immediately the Spirit drove him out into	1
	the wilderness.	
1:13	And he was in the wilderness forty days,	3
	tempted by Satan;	2
	and he was with the wild beasts,	—
	and the angels ministered to him.	—

5   no. 4a

1:14	And after John was delivered up,	—
	Jesus came into Galilee,	1
1:15	preaching the gospel of God, and saying,	2
	"The time is fulfilled,	—
	and the kingdom of God is at hand;	—
	repent,	—
	and believe in the gospel."	

6   no. 5

13:9	But take heed to yourselves;	—
	for they will deliver you up to councils;	10
	and you will be beaten in synagogues;	11
	and you will stand before governors and kings	12, 13
	for my sake,	
	to bear testimony before them.	—

7   no. 7

4:24	And he said to them,	—
	"Take heed what you hear;	—
	the measure you give will be the measure you get,	10
	and still more will be given you."	—

8   no. 15

1:2	(As it is written in Isaiah the prophet,)	12
	"Behold, I send my messenger before your face,	13
	who shall prepare your way."	14

Mk	9	Q no. 18
6:6b	And he went about among the villages teaching.	—
6:7	And he called to him the twelve,	1
	and began to send them out two by two,	2
	and gave them authority over the unclean spirits,	—
6:8	and he charged them	3
	to take nothing for their journey except a staff;	no. 21:1
	no bread, no bag, no money in their belts;	
6:9	but to wear sandals	—
	and not put on two tunics.	—
6:10	And he said to them,	—
	"Where you enter a house,	3
	stay there until you leave the place.	8
6:11	And if any place will not receive you	17, 18
	and they refuse to hear you,	—
	when you leave there,	19
	shake off the dust that is on your feet	20
	for a testimony against them."	—
6:12	And they went out and preached that people should repent,	—
6:13	and they cast out many demons	—
	and anointed with oil many that were sick	—
	and healed.	—

Mk	10	no. 23
9:37	Whoever receives one such child in my name,	1
	receives me;	
	and whoever receives me,	3
	receives not me but him who sent me.	

Mk	11	no. 29
3:22	And the scribes who came down from Jerusalem said,	5
	"He is possessed by Beelzebul,	6
	and by the prince of demons	
	he casts out the demons."	7
3:23	And he called them to him, and said to them in parables,	8

Mk		Q
	"How can Satan cast out Satan?	—
3:24	and if a kingdom is divided against itself,	9
	that kingdom cannot stand.	
3:25	And if a house is divided against itself,	10
	that house will not be able to stand.	
3:26	And if Satan has risen up against himself and	11
	is divided,	
	he cannot stand, but is coming to an end."	12

	12	no. 30
3:27	But no one can enter a strong man's house	1,2
	and plunder his goods,	
	unless the strong man is first bound;	3
	then indeed his house may be plundered.	5

	13	no. 33
8:11	And the Pharisees came	1
	and began to argue with him,	—
	seeking from him a sign from heaven,	2
	testing him.	—
8:12	And sighing deeply in his spirit, he said,	3
	"Why does this generation seek a sign?	4,5
	Truly, I say to you,	—
	no sign shall be given to this generation."	5

	14	no. 35
4:21	And he said to them,	—
	"Is a lamp brought in	1
	to be put under a bushel or under a bed	2
	and not put on a stand?"	3

	15	no. 36
12:38	And in his teaching he said,	—
	"Beware of the scribes,	12
	who like to go about in long robes,	—
	and to have salutations in the market places	14
12:39	and the best seats in the synagogues	13
	and the places of honor at feasts,	—
12:40	who devour widows' houses	—
	and for a pretense make long prayers.	—
	They will receive the greater condemnation."	—

	16	no. 36a
8:15	And he cautioned them, saying,	
	"Take heed,	—

Mk		Q
	beware of the leaven of the Pharisees and the leaven of Herod."	1 —
	17	no. 37
4:22	For there is nothing hid, except to be made manifest; nor is anything secret, except to come to light.	1 2 3 4
4:23	If any have ears to hear, let them hear.	(59:6)
	18	no. 39
8:38	For whoever is ashamed of me and of my words in this adulterous and sinful generation, the son of man will also be ashamed of that one, when he comes in the glory of his Father with the holy angels.	4 5
	19	no. 40
3:28	Truly, I say to you, all will be forgiven the sons of men— the sins and blasphemies, whatever they blaspheme;	— 2 1
3:29	but whoever blasphemes against the holy Spirit, never has forgiveness but is guilty of an eternal sin.	3 4 —
	20	no. 41
13:11	And when they bring you to trial and deliver you up, do not be anxious beforehand what you are to say; but whatever is given you in that hour, say this, for it is not you who speak, but the holy Spirit.	1 2 3 4 — 3
	21	no. 45/46
13:33	Take heed, watch, for you do not know when the time will come.	45:1,2 —
13:34	It is like a man going on a journey, when he leaves home and puts his servants in charge, each with his work, and commands the doorkeeper to be on the watch.	45:3 (47:2) (75:2) —

Mk		Q
13:35	Watch therefore—	45:5
	for you do not know when the master of the house will come,	46:5
	in the evening, or at midnight, or at cockcrow, or in the morning—	46:6
13:36	lest he come suddenly and find you asleep.	45:11
13:37	And what I say to you, I say to all: Watch!	45:7

	22	no. 48
13:12	And brother will deliver up brother to death, and the father his child,	8,9
	and children will rise against parents	7
	and have them put to death.	(6)

	23	no. 52
4:30	And he said,	
	"With what can we compare the kingdom of God,	1
	or what parable shall we use for it?	2
4:31	It is like a grain of mustard seed,	3
	which, when sown upon the ground,	4
	is the smallest of all the seeds on earth;	—
4:32	yet when it is sown, it grows up	5
	and becomes the greatest of all shrubs,	—
	and puts forth large branches,	6
	so that the birds of the air can make their nests in its shade."	6

	24	no. 56
10:31	But many that are first will be last,	2
	and the last first.	1

	25	no. 58
8:34	And having called to him the multitude with his disciples,	
	he said to them,	
	"If anyone would come after me,	1,6
	let that one deny self	—
	and take up the cross	5
	and follow me."	7

	26	no. 59
9:49	For everyone will be salted with fire.	—
9:50	Salt is good;	1
	but if the salt has lost its saltiness,	2

Mk		Q
	how will you season it?	3
	Have salt in yourselves,	—
	and be at peace with one another.	—
	27	no. 64
10:11	And he said to them,	—
	"Whoever divorces his wife and marries another,	1
	commits adultery against her;	2
10:12	and if she divorces her husband and marries another,	3
	she commits adultery."	4
	28	no. 66
9:42	Whoever causes one of these little ones who believe in me to stumble,	2,6
	it would be better for that person,	3
	if a great millstone were hung round the neck,	4
	and that one were thrown into the sea.	5
	29	no. 68
11:22	And Jesus answered them,	
	"Have faith in God.	1
11:23	Truly, I say to you,	—
	whoever says to this mountain,	2
	'Be taken up and cast into the sea,'	3
	and does not doubt in the heart,	—
	but believes that what is said will come to pass,	—
	it will be done for that one."	4
	30	no. 69
13:21	And then if anyone says to you,	1
	"Look, here is the Christ!" or	2
	"Look, there he is!"	4
	do not believe it.	5
	31	no. 71
13:14c	Then let those who are in Judea flee to the mountains,	—
	let whoever is on the housetop	
13:15	not go down, nor enter the house, to take anything away;	1
	and let whoever is in the field	2
13:16	not turn back to take one's mantle.	3

Mk		Q
	32	no. 72
8:35	For whoever would save one's life	1
	will lose it;	2
	and whoever loses one's life	3
	for my sake and the gospel's	—
	will save it.	4
	33	no. 75
4:25	For to one who has will more be given,	29
	and from the one who has not, even what	30
	that one has will be taken away.	

SYNOPSIS OF Mk AND Q TRADITIONS

	Mk-Tradition			Q-Tradition		
no.	**Mk**	**Mt**	**Lk**	**Q no.**	**Mt**	**Lk**
1	1:2-5	3:1-3,5,6	3:2b-4	1	3:1-3,5b	3:2b-4
2	1:7,8	3:11	3:16	2	3:7-12	3:7-17
3	1:9-11	3:13,16,17	3:21,22	3	3:13,16,17	3:21,22
4	1:12,13	4:1,2,11	4:1,2	4	4:1-11	4:1-13
5	1:14,15	4:11,12,17	—	4a	4:12b,13	4:14,15
					4:23,24a	
6	13:9	⌈ 24:9; ⌊ 10:17,18	21:12,13	5	5:11	6:22
7	4:24	—	(8:18a)	7	7:2b	6:38b
8	1:2	—	—	15	11:10	7:27
9	6:6b-13	⌈ 9:35;10:1 ⌊ 10:9,11,14	9:1-6	⌈18 ⌊21	— 10:7-15	10:1 10:4-12
10	9:37	18:5	9:48	23	10:40	10:16
11	3:22-26	12:24-26	—	29	12:22-28	11:14-20
12	3:27	12:29	—	30	—	11:21,22
13	8:11,12	16:1,4	—	33	12:38-40	11:29,30
14	4:21	—	8:16	35	5:15	11:33
15	12:38-40	23:6a	20:45-47	36	23:6,7	11:43
16	8:15	16:6	—	36a	—	12:1b

no.	Mk	Mt	Lk	Q no.	Mt	Lk
17	4:22,23	—	8:17	37	10:26	12:2
18	8:38	16:27	9:26	39	10:32,33	12:8,9
19	3:28,29	12:31,32	—	40	12:32	12:10
20	13:11	10:19,20	21:14,15	41	10:19	12:11,12
21	13:33-37	24:42; (25:13)	—	⌐45	—	12:35-38
				└46	24:43,44	12:39,40
22	13:12	10:21	21:16	48	10:34-36	12:51-53
23	4:30-32	13:31,32	—	52	13:31,32	13:18,19
24	10:31	19:30	—	56	20:16	13:30
25	8:34	16:24	9:23	58	10:37,38	14:26,27
26	9:49,50	—	—	59	5:13	14:34,35
27	10:11,12	19:9	—	64	5:32	16:18
28	9:42	18:6	—	66	18:6,7	17:1,2
29	11:22,23	21:21	—	68	17:20	17:6
30	13:21	24:23	—	69	24:26	17:23
31	13:14-16	24:16-18	21:21	71	—	17:31,32
32	8:35	16:25	9:24	72	10:39	17:33
33	4:25	13:12	8:18b	75	25:29	19:26

Appendix IV.

SEPTUAGINT PASSAGES APPEARING IN Q

	cf. Q no. 1:4-6
Isa 40:3	A voice of one crying in the wilderness, "Prepare the way of the Lord; make straight the paths of our God."
	cf. Q no. 3:6-7
Ps 2:7	The Lord said to me, "You are my son; today have I begotten you."
Isa 42:1	Jacob is my servant, I will help him; Israel is my chosen, my soul has accepted him; I have put my Spirit upon him; he shall bring forth judgment to the Gentiles.
(Isa 44:2b)	(My servant Jacob and beloved Israel, whom I have chosen)
(Ex 4:22b)	(Israel is my first born son.)
(Gen 22:2a)	(Take your son, the beloved one, whom you have loved...)
(Jer 38:20 LXX)	(Ephraim is a beloved son of mine, a pleasing child...)
	cf. Q no. 4:10
Dt 8:3b	...that one shall not live by bread alone but one shall live by every word that proceeds out of the mouth of God.

cf. Q 4:17-19

Ps 90:11-12 LXX   For he shall give his angels charge over you
to keep you in all your ways;/
they shall bear you up on their hands,
lest at any time you dash your foot against a
stone.

cf. Q no 4:22

Dt 6:16   You shall not tempt the Lord your God,
as you tempted him in the temptation.

cf. Q no. 4:30-31

Dt 6:13a   You shall fear the Lord your God,
and him shall you serve.

cf. Q no. 14:7-9

Isa 61:1-2   The Spirit of the Lord is upon me, because he
has anointed me;
he has sent me to preach good news to the poor,
to heal the broken in heart,
to proclaim liberty to the captives, and recovery
of sight to the blind,/
to declare the acceptable year of the Lord and
the day of recompense,
to comfort all that mourn.

Isa 42:6b-7   And I have given you for the covenant of a race,
for a light of the Gentiles;/
to open the eyes of the blind,
to bring the bound out of bonds,
and those that sit in darkness out of the prison-
house.

Isa 35:5-6a   Then shall the eyes of the blind be opened,
and the ears of the deaf shall hear./
Then shall the lame man leap as an hart,
and the tongue of the stammerers shall speak
plainly.

Isa 29:18-19a   And in that day the deaf shall hear the words of
the book,
and the eyes of the blind that are in darkness
and in the mist shall see,/
and the poor shall rejoice
with joy because of the Lord.

Isa 26:19a	The dead shall rise, and they that are in the tombs shall be raised, and they that are in the earth shall rejoice.
	cf. Q no. 15:13
Mal 3:1a	Behold, I send forth my messenger, and he shall survey the way before me.
	cf. Q no. 22:8-9
Isa 14:13a, 15	But you said in your heart, "I will go up to heaven,". . ./ But now you shall go down to hell, even to the foundations of the earth.
	cf. Q no. 48:7-11
Mic 7:6	For the son dishonors his father, the daughter will rise up against her mother, the daughter-in-law against her mother-in-law; all those who are in his house shall be enemies of the man.
	cf. Q no. 51:7
Jer 22:5	But if you will not perform these words, by myself have I sworn, says the Lord, this house shall be brought to desolation.
	cf. Q no. 51:9
Ps 117:26 LXX	Blessed is he that comes in the name of the Lord; we have blessed you from the house of the Lord.
	cf. Q no. 52:6
Ps 103:12 LXX	By them shall the birds of the sky lodge; they shall utter a voice out of the midst of the rocks.
	cf. Q no. 54:11
Ps 6:9a	Depart from me, all you who work iniquity.

SELECT BIBLIOGRAPHY

A. *Non-Technical Works on Q in English* (Annotated)

Beare, Francis Wright. *The Earliest Records of Jesus.* A *Companion to the Synopsis of the First Three Gospels by Albert Huck.* New York and Nashville: Abingdon Press, 1962. This does not treat Q separately but does give a brief commentary on the parallel passages of Matthew and Luke that belong to Q.

Crum, J.M.C. *The Original Jerusalem Gospel. Being Essays on the Document Q.* London: Constable & Company, LTD, 1927. This early work on Q perceptively deals with topics that are now standard concerns of Q research. It includes an English reconstruction of the text of Q, pp. 128–166.

Davies, W.D. *The Setting of the Sermon on the Mount.* Cambridge: Cambridge University Press, 1966. This book contains a chapter entitled "Q and Crisis; Catechesis; the Pastorals," pp. 366–386, which is significant for movement away from the older idea that Q materials were merely ethical, catechetical instruction.

Edwards, Richard A. *A Theology of Q. Eschatology, Prophecy, and Wisdom.* Philadelphia: Fortress Press, 1976. This book presents the major concerns of Q theology together with commentary on the parallel passages. It is the most complete and up to date of recent non-technical discussions of Q in English and it has an excellent bibliography.

Hunter, Archibald M.   *The Work and Words of Jesus.* rev. ed. Philadelphia: The Westminster Press, 1973. This presents a running commentary on the life and teachings of Jesus, taking note of Q materials but not as separate subject matter. It does contain, however, a reconstruction of Q in English, pp. 165–180.

Kee, Howard Clark.   *Jesus in History. An Approach to the Study of the Gospels.* 2nd ed. New York: Harcourt Brace Jovanovich, Inc., 1977. This introduction to the biblical Gospels contains a chapter dedicated exclusively to Q, analyzing its materials, theology and community, pp. 76–120.

Kelber, Werner H.   *The Oral and the Written Gospel. The Hermeneutics of Speaking and Writing in the Synoptic Tradition, Mark, Paul, and Q.* Philadelphia: Fortress Press, 1983. Although Q is dealt with in only a few scattered pages, this book nonetheless is an important step forward in defining the Q community and the oral nature of the Q document itself.

Kingsbury, Jack Dean.   *Jesus Christ in Matthew, Mark, and Luke*, in: *Proclamation Commentaries.* Philadelphia: Fortress Press, 1981. The first chapter of this book, pp. 1–27, provides a look at the theological content of Q and some helpful insights into the Q community.

Manson, T.W.   *The Sayings of Jesus.* Grand Rapids: William B. Eerdmans Publishing Company, 1979 [= Part II of *The Mission and Message of Jesus.* London: SCM Press, 1937]. This is one of the more detailed commentaries on Q in English. While the text of Q is not reconstructed, the appropriate parallels in Matthew and Luke are carefully analyzed, pp. 39–148. Although it is an older work, it is still a useful resource.

Neirynck, Frans. "Q," *The Interpreter's Dictionary of the Bible. Supplementary Volume.* Nashville: Abingdon Press, 1976. Pp. 715–716. A brief but helpful overview of key issues concerning Q.

B. *Technical Works on Q in English (or English Translation)*

[Some knowledge of Greek is presupposed for effective use of these resources.]

Boring, M. Eugene. *Sayings of the Risen Jesus. Christian Prophecy in the Synoptic Tradition,* in: *Society for New Testament Studies, Monograph Series,* 46. Cambridge: Cambridge University Press, 1982.

Crossan, John Dominic. *In Fragments. The Aphorisms of Jesus.* San Francisco: Harper & Row, Publishers, 1983.

Edwards, Richard A. *A Concordance to Q,* in: *SBL Sources for Biblical Study,* 7. Chico, CA: Scholars Press, 1975.

Harnack, Adolf. *New Testament Studies II. The Sayings of Jesus. The Second Source of St. Matthew and St. Luke,* in: *Crown Theological Library,* 23. Trans. J.R. Wilkinson. New York: G.P. Putnam's Sons, 1908.

Jacobson, Arland Dean. *Wisdom Christology in Q.* diss. Claremont Graduate School, 1978 (= Ann Arbor, MI and London: University Microfilms International, 1981).

Meyer, Paul Donald. *The Community of Q.* diss. University of Iowa, 1967 [Chapter II published separately: "The Gentile Mission in Q," *Journal of Biblical Literature,* 89 (1970), 405–417].

Robinson, James M. and Koester, Helmut. *Trajectories through Early Christianity.* Philadelphia: Fortress Press, 1971.

Tödt, Heinz Edward. *The Son of Man in the Synoptic Tradition*, in: *The New Testament Library*. Trans. Dorothea M. Barton. Philadelphia: The Westminster Press, 1965.

Worden, Ronald D. "Redaction Criticism of Q: A Survey," *Journal of Biblical Literature*, 94 (1975), 532–546.

C.   *Major Foreign Language Works on Q*

Bussmann, Wilhelm. *Synoptische Studien II. Zur Redenquelle*. Halle, 1929.

Delobel, Joël. ed. *Logia. Les paroles de Jésus—The Sayings of Jesus*, in: *Bibliotheca Ephemeridum Theologicarum Lovaniensium*, 59. Leuven: Leuven University Press, 1982.

Hoffmann, Paul. *Studien zur Theologie der Logienquelle*, in: *Neutestamentliche Abhandlungen*, Neue Folge, 8. Münster: Verlag Aschendorff, 1972.

Laufen, Rudolf. *Die Doppelüberlieferungen der Logienquelle und des Markusevangeliums*, in: *Bonner Biblische Beiträge*, 54. Königstein/Ts.-Bonn: Verlag Peter Hanstein, 1980.

Lührman, Dieter. *Die Redaktion der Logienquelle*, in: *Wissenschaftliche Monographien zum Alten und Neuen Testament*, 33. Neukirchen-Vluyn: Neukirchener Verlag, 1969.

Polag, Athanasius. *Die Christologie der Logienquelle,* in: *Wissenschaftliche Monographien zum Alten und Neuen Testament*, 45. Neukirchen-Vluyn: Neukirchener Verlag, 1977.

——————. *Fragmenta Q. Textheft zur Logienquelle*. Neukirchen-Vluyn: Neukirchener Verlag 1979; 2 ed. with corrections, 1982.

Schenk, Wolfgang. *Synopse zur Redenquelle der Evangelien. Q—Synopse und Rekonstruktion in deutscher Übersetzung mit kurzen Erläuterungen*. Düsseldorf: Patmos Verlag, 1981.

Schulz, Siegfried. *Griechisch-deutsche Synopse der Q—Überlieferungen*. Zurich: Theologischer Verlag Zürich, 1972.

_____. *Q. Die Spruchquelle der Evangelisten*. Zurich: Theologischer Verlag Zürich, 1972.

Segalla, Giuseppe. "La cristologia escatologica della *Quelle*," *Teologia*, 4 (1979), 119-168.

Soiron, Thaddaeus. *Die Logia Jesu. Eine literarkritische und literargeschichtliche Untersuchung zum synoptischen Problem*, in: *Neutestamentliche Abhandlungen*, 6, Heft 4. Münster: Aschendorffsche Verlagsbuchhandlung, 1916.

Vielhauer, Philipp. "Die Spruchquelle," *Geschichte der urchristlichen Literatur*, in: *de Gruyter Lehrbuch*. Berlin and New York: Walter de Gruyter, 1975. Pp. 311-329.

Zeller, Dieter. *Kommentar zur Logienquelle*, in: *Stuttgarter Kleiner Kommentar, Neues Testament*, 21. Stuttgart: Verlag Katholisches Bibelwerk, 1984.

Index of Ancient Writings

Q References

For a listing of all the Matthaean and Lucan passages in Q, see pp. 117-122. For a synopsis of Marcan and Q traditions, see pp. 160-161. Text of Q, pp. 123-146.

Individual Passages

Q.

1	43, 63, 84	32	86
2	53, 57, 63, 85, 87, 88, 90, 96, 101	33	72, 99
		34	83
3	34-35, 46, 48, 63, 64, 68, 87, 88	36	36, 48, 79, 81, 82, 98-99
		38	36-37, 48
4	35-36, 43, 46, 48, 49, 68, 88, 90	39	46, 59, 72, 73, 89, 90
		40	51 n. 41; 72, 88-89, 90
5-12	69	41	48, 90, 98
5-13	65	42	43, 59, 60, 72, 97-98
5	38, 54, 69, 72, 95-96	43	47, 98
6	70, 71, 96-97	44	54
7	48	45	61
9	38	46	59, 60, 61, 72
10	65	47	61, 85
12	70, 83	48	93 n. 76
13	34, 43, 84, 100-101	51	40, 43, 79, 81, 82, 85, 98, 102
14-16	65	52	37, 52
14	51, 63, 64-65, 70	54	85
15	48, 63, 65, 80, 83	55	49, 55, 101
16	63, 66, 72, 79, 97	57	54-55, 102
17-25	58, 72	58	32 n. 24; 93
17-28	92	60	98
17	84, 92-93	61	37, 49
18	43, 58, 85	62	51, 63, 98
19	39	63	46, 48, 98
20	43, 97	64	39
21	52-53, 58-59, 94	65	49
22	43, 59	67	39
23	71, 95	69	38-39, 59, 72
24	46, 71, 79, 80, 88	70	59, 61, 72
25	71, 98	73	38
26	49, 55, 98	75	61, 85
28	48		
29	33, 50, 70		

Matthew

7:7-11	40
10:5b	97
10:23	97
13:31-32	26
14:1-12	66 n. 50
23:37-39	24
26:1-5	20
28:19-20	62

Mark

For Marcan parallels to Q, see pp. 153-160. For a synopsis of Marcan and Q traditions, see pp. 160-161.

1:12-13	35
4:30-32	26
6:14-29	66 n. 50
9:31	73
14:1-2	20

Luke

1:1-4	17
3:19-20	66 n. 50
9:7-9	66 n. 50
10:29-37	37
11:9-13	40
11:14-26	29
13:18-19	26
13:34-35	24
15:11-32	37
22:1-2	20

John

1:29-31	67 n. 51
3:27-30	67 n. 51

Acts

1-28	44
1:8	62
7:56	72
20:35	29 n. 17; 30

1 Thess.

1:9-10	107

Hebrews

2:6	72

Apocalypse

1-22	76
1:13	72
14:14	72

For Septuagint passages appearing in Q, see pp. 163-165.

Proverbs	78
Wisdom	78
Sirach	78
Isaiah	51, 83
Baruch	78
Daniel	
7:13	74, 75
Anti-Marcionite Prologue	44 n. 38
Barnabas	
12:10	72
Didache	43
1 Enoch	74, 75, 78
4 Esdras	74, 75, 78
Eusebius, *Church History II* 23, 13	72
Ignatius, *Ephesians* 20:2	72
Gospel of Peter	18
Gospel of Thomas	18, 29 n. 17; 30, 31, 44-45

Index of Selected Topics, Persons and Places

Antioch, 44

Aramaic, 45, 74, 75 n. 60

Bethsaida, 43, 59

Capernaum, 43, 59

Christ (definition), 68

Christian-Jews, 46, 56, 103, 105-106

Chorazin, 43, 59

demon (s), 33, 50, 51 n. 41; 66, 70, 71, 86-87

devil, 35-36, 48, 68-69, 70, 88, 90

disciples, a) of Jesus, 42 also n. 34; 43, 52, 58, 60, 62, 73, 87, 90, 91, 92-93, 94-95, 96, 100; b) of John the Baptist, 62, 64-65, 67

eschatological banquet, 54-56, 77, 101

exorcism (s), 50-51, 70, 91

Father (designation for God), 46, 47, 48, 49, 71, 80, 82, 84, 85-86, 88, 89

Galilee, 43, 44, 45

Gentile (s), 56, 97, 98, 99, 100, 101, 102, 105, 106; cities (Tyre and Sidon), 43

Gnostic/Gnosticism, 31, 72

God, 45-50, 54, 63, 64, 68, 78, 80, 84, 85-86, 89, 102, 105

healing (s), 52, 58, 65, 91, 100

infancy narratives, 23, 64

Israel, 43, 60, 63, 78, 95, 96, 97, 98, 101, 102, 103, 105

Jerusalem, 43, 62, 81, 82, 98, 102

Jesus, a) preaching, 42, 52-53, 58, 63, 65, 69, 70, 74, 81, 91; b) ministry (related to the kingdom of God), 50-62; c) relation to John the Baptist, 62-67; d) death, 32, 42, 71, 106; e) resurrection, 42, 56, 73, 74, 77, 85, 106; f) as an apocalyptic figure, 42, 53, 56, 59, 60, 67, 76-77, 85; g) as a prophet, 66, 68, 69, 71, 77, 82, 83, 84 n. 68; 95; h) as son of man, 72-77; i) as Wisdom's agent, 55, 78-83, 105; j) as Lord, 46, 82-86; k) as God's prophetic Son, 49-50, 64, 68-71, 72, 77, 82-83, 87, 88, 89, 90, 105

Jewish War, 45

Jews, 46, 96, 97, 98, 99, 100, 101, 102, 103, 105, 106

John the Baptist, 51, 53, 56, 57, 58, 59, 62-67, 68, 70, 77, 79, 82, 83, 84, 87, 88, 89, 90, 96, 98, 99, 101, 104-105

Jordan, 43, 63

judgment, 49, 50, 55, 56, 57-62, 63, 76, 81, 85, 87, 96, 98, 99, 106

kingdom of God, 32, 42, 48, 50-62, 66, 69, 70, 71, 74, 76, 77, 101, 102, 103; a) definition, 50; b) present in ministry of Jesus, 50-53; c) future manifestation, 53-57; d) relation to judgment 56, 57-62

logia, 29

Lord (designation for Jesus), 46, 83-86

midrash (definition), 75

Messiah (definition), 68

parousia, 60-61, 73 (definition), 74, 75

passion narrative, 32

Paul, 11, 30, 72, 76, 84, 86, 103, 106

pericope (definition), 19

Peter, 43, 44

prophets (of the Q community), 31-32, 42, 56, 60, 69-70, 77, 87, 90, 94-95, 96, 98, 103-104, 106

Q, a) names, 19, 28-29; b) hypothesis, 19-28; c) genre, 29-30; d) oral nature, 32-36, 40; e) forms of the sayings, 36-39; f) date, 42-43, 45; g) place of composition, 43-45; h) primary theological thrust, 67; i) way of salvation, 71; j) interest in apocalyptic, 67; k) not a biblical document, 11-12; see also the table of contents of this volume for key topics of Q and the nature of the Q community and its mission

Quelle, 28

realized (or present) eschatology, 50

Rome, 62

repentance, 42, 49, 53, 57, 59, 63-64, 68, 87, 99, 100, 103

resurrection narratives, 23

Satan, 33, 35, 50

"sayings" genre, 29-31

Septuagint (LXX), 45, 51

sermon on the mount, 23, 65, 96

Sidon, 43, 59

Son of God, 68-71

son of man, 53, 54, 56, 59, 60, 67, 69, 72-77, 89, 98, 99, 105

Spirit, 48, 51 n. 41; 58, 63, 65, 68, 69, 86-91

Synoptic Gospels, a) definition, 19; b) priority of Mark, 19-24; c) minor agreements between Matthew and Luke, 23; d) special M and L, 24, 25, 44-45, 60, 61; 3) two source hypothesis, 25; relation of Mark to Q, 26, also n. 12; 27

Syria, a) western, 43, 44, 45; b) eastern, 44, 45

theology (definition), 45

"this generation", 66, 79, 81, 82, 97, 98, 99, 100

Thomas, 44

Tyre, 43, 59

Wisdom, 48, 55, 66, 78-83, 85, 90 n. 72; 98, 99, 102, 103, 105

Index of Modern Authors

Beardslee, William A, 23 n. 8 & 10
Beare, Francis Wright, 54, n. 42
Beasley-Murray, George R., 75 n.61
Boring, M. Eugene, 29 n. 17; 38 n. 30
Borsch, Frederick Houk, 72 n. 55
Bousset, Wilhelm, 28
Bultmann, Rudolf, 32 n. 26; 112
Cameron, Ron, 18 n. 3; 30 n. 25
Carlston, Charles E., 37 n. 29; 78 also n. 64; 79 n. 65
Carruth, Shawn, 44 n. 40
Christ, Felix, 79 n. 65
Crossan, John Dominic, 37 n. 28
Crum, J.M.C., 64 n. 49
Dillon, Richard, 95 n. 79
Duncan, Robert L. (=James Hall Roberts), 18
Dungan, David, 30 n. 20
Edwards, Richard A., 37 n. 29; 38 n. 30
Fuller, Reginald H., 44 n. 38; 74 n. 58; 84 n. 68
Farmer, William R., 22
Hahn, Ferdinand, 74 n. 58
Hansen, T., 23 n. 9
Harnack, Adolf, 64 n. 49; 112
Havener, Ivan, 68 n. 52; 107 n. 93
Hoffmann, Paul, 57 n. 45; 97 n. 81
Howard, W.F., 28 n. 13
Hunter, Archibald M., 64 n. 49
Jacobson, Arland Dean, 51 n. 41; 63 n. 47; 64 n. 48-49; 75 n. 61; 79 n. 65; 82 n. 67; 87 n. 70; 89 n. 71
Kee, Howard Clark, 33 n. 26
Kelber, Werner H., 30 n. 20; 31 n. 21-22; 32 also n. 23 & 25; 40 n. 31; 91 n. 73; 92 also n. 74-75; 94 n. 77-78; 104 also n. 90-91

Kingsbury, Jack Dean, 43, n. 35
Kloppenborg, John, 79 n. 65; 81 n. 66
Koester, Helmut, 43 n. 36-37; 44 n. 39-40
Kümmel, Werner Georg, 21 n. 6
Laufen, Rudolf, 26 n. 12
Lührmann, Dieter, 57 n. 45
McArthur, Harvey K., 29 n. 16
Manson, T.W., 74 n. 59
Meyer, Paul Donald, 55 n. 43; 99 n. 82; 100 n. 83; 101 n. 84 & 86; 102 n. 87; 103 n. 88-89
Neirynck, Frans, 23 n. 9; 29 n. 16
Nickelsburg, George W.E., 75 n.61
Polag, Athanasius, 12; 13; 19; 25 n. 11; 42 n. 33; 58; 59; 62; 64 n. 49; 84 n. 69; 88; 92; 97
Roberts, James Hall (=Robert L. Duncan), 18
Robinson, J. Armitage, 28
Robinson, James M., 12; 29 n. 17; 30 n. 18
Schulz, Siegfried, 51 n. 41
Schürmann, Heinz, 42 n. 33; 112
Scobie, H.H., 62 n. 46
Silbermann, Lou H., 28 n. 14
Theissen, Gerd, 91 n. 73
Tödt, Heinz Eduard, 73 n. 56; 74 n. 58; 105
Van Segbroeck, F., 23 n. 9
Vermes, Geza, 75 n. 60; 105
Vielhauer, Philipp, 56 n. 44; 74 n. 57
Wallace, Irving, 18
Weiss, Johannes, 28-29
Wellhausen, Julius, 28
Wernle, Paul, 28
Zeller, Dieter, 41 n. 32; 106 n. 92